The Mirror of Antiquity

The Mirror of Antiquity
20th Century British Travellers in Greece

By

David Wills

CAMBRIDGE SCHOLARS PUBLISHING

The Mirror of Antiquity: 20th Century British Travellers in Greece, by David Wills

This book first published 2007 by

Cambridge Scholars Publishing

15 Angerton Gardens, Newcastle, NE5 2JA, UK

British Library Cataloguing in Publication Data
A catalogue record for this book is available from the British Library

ISBN 1-84718-267-4; ISBN 13: 9781847182678

The Philhellenes are not calculable; the travellers are diverse, only the spell under which they return is the same. And the passion is ineradicable. These are lovers who never escape into satiety, indifference and the shabby world of the familiar.

—Dilys Powell, *The Traveller's Journey is Done*

That is Greece, a country where the fabric of legend jostles the pedestrian.

—Ian Brook, *A Sea Blue Boat, and a Sun God's Island*

TABLE OF CONTENTS

LIST OF TABLES

FOREWORD

Britons have been travelling to Greek lands and recording their experiences since the sixteenth century. Their accounts, and those of their successors in subsequent centuries, preserve much valuable information about what they encountered on their journeys: the terrain, climate, flora and fauna, the visible remains of past civilisations, and of course the people who inhabited the Greek landscape, their appearance and dress, way of life, customs and beliefs, and much more. In more recent times most people with an interest in Greece will have read and profited from the "classic" travel works of writers of the calibre of Dilys Powell, Lawrence Durrell and Patrick Leigh Fermor.

We might therefore be tempted to assume that travel writings offer an objective and reliable source of information about Greece over the last four centuries or more. That would be to take for granted that we know what we mean by "Greece", and that there is such a thing as objective travel writing. "Greece" is a slippery term. Until the creation of the modern state it had no fixed geographical applicability and even after that the boundaries continued to change for more than a hundred years. The other problem we face is that the words "Greece" and "Greek" are frequently used without qualification to refer to the history and culture of a number of city-states that flourished two and a half millennia ago. This slippage is with us still (classicists teach Greek, but I must say I teach *Modern* Greek); Richard Clogg's *A Concise History of Greece*, which begins with the eighteenth-century stirrings that would eventually lead to independence, is the exception that proves the rule.

Until the middle of the last century a good education involved, more often than not, the study of Greek and Latin. It was inevitable that travellers to classical lands should relate their contemporary observations to their knowledge of the civilisations that had formerly flourished on the same territory. David Wills shows this very clearly in his central chapters examining the bountiful harvest of 92 travel books on Greece, published in Britain between 1940 and 1974. Consciously or unconsciously, most of these writers make constant comparisons between their own encounters in Greece and historical or mythical persons and events familiar from the ancient world. Their prior knowledge, therefore, creates certain expectations and exerts an influence on what they notice or fail to notice. The study of travel writing should not stop at the analysis of the ostensible factual content of the text, but engage too with the author. His or her preconceptions, prejudices, preferences and tastes—cultural, political, religious or whatever—are a vital element of the process of writing and need to be "read" with a sensitive awareness of all the potential issues. It is this attention to the importance of reading between the lines, of analysing the "gaze" of the travel writer, that distinguishes David Wills's fascinating and original study from most previous work on travel writing about Greece.

While these travellers to Greece cannot resist reminding us of the glory that *was* Greece, they are often surprisingly well-informed about current social, economic and political realities, never more so than in the years that followed Greece's entry into the Second World War. Again it is not just a matter of what they saw, but of what they chose to notice, how they interpreted their experiences and how they related them to wider political considerations. With the increasing impact of the West and of modernity on traditional Greek society since the 1970s, much has inevitably changed. Much that the traveller and the travel writer once found quaint, charming, primitive or "oriental", or seized on as evidence of continuity since ancient times, has disappeared from view. The enormous growth in tourism has left only the remotest corners untouched. But the travel writers have also changed. They are much less likely now to possess a deep knowledge of classical culture, but neither can they assume that their readers will be well-informed on matters of ancient history, literature or myth. The range of interests exhibited by travel writers of the last thirty years is in fact broader, more encompassing of everyday life with all its varieties of experience, pleasure, *aporia* and irritation. In part this is because many of these travel writers have settled permanently in Greece, or at least spent more than a couple of weeks' holiday there. Although the classical Greek world has certainly not ceased to exercise a fascination and indeed to impinge significantly on current social and political realities (examples are obvious), it is no longer central to the interests of travel writers. Shelley's claim that "we are all Greeks" is less easy to support, in a world that is only dimly aware of the huge debt that Western civilisation owes to the achievements of the ancient Greeks. Motives for travelling to, and writing about, Greece have varied widely, but it is clear that many of these authors were (also) engaging in a process of self-discovery. By forsaking, for a time, their familiar routines and surroundings and seeking to understand an unfamiliar "Other", they were, consciously or not, exploring their own identity and, through that reflective process, revealing to the reader more than they realised. Travel writing about Greece may indeed serve as a "mirror of Antiquity", but it also allows us to observe, as David Wills demonstrates, the attitudes and preoccupations of the authors themselves.

David Holton
Selwyn College, Cambridge

ACKNOWLEDGEMENTS

The research upon which this book draws was originally conducted for my PhD thesis under the supervision of Professor John Eade and Dr Garry Marvin (University of Surrey Roehampton, 2003). My old friends Dr Eleana Yalouri and Dr Karl Strobl encouraged me in the belief that the study of travel writing about Greece was a workable area for research. During the course of my formal studies, and since, I have received encouragement and support in particular from: my parents, John and Margaret Wills; Simon and Briony Holland; Sandy Kirby; and my colleagues in the History department at Newlands Girls' School in Maidenhead.

I am grateful to various audiences who have allowed me to try out my ideas and made useful comments and suggestions. In particular, my thanks to Professors David Holton and Roderick Beaton for their invitations to contribute to lecture series at Cambridge and King's College London respectively. I was delighted that Professor Holton agreed to write the foreword to this book. Dr Tim Duff was kind enough to introduce me to Cambridge Scholars Publishing. Dr Christopher Stray and Dr Mike Morse offered valuable advice on the final form of this work. I am grateful to Lorie Jones for editorial assistance. None of the above named bear responsibility for my work, and cannot be assumed to share my opinions.

In addition to travel literature in my own collection, books and publications used in this research were consulted at the University Library, Cambridge; the Joint Library of the Hellenic and Roman Societies, London; University of Surrey Roehampton; and the British Library.

Some material in this book has previously been published in different forms. It is reused courtesy of Johns Hopkins University Press (Wills 2005a); The White Horse Press (Wills 2005b); and the Faculty of Modern and Medieval Languages, University of Cambridge (Wills 2006).

INTRODUCTION

Greece occupies a unique place in the British geographical imagination. For much of the twentieth century, the literary representation of travel to Greece was remarkably consistent. In this book I aim to explain why.

Writers as diverse as fairy tale exponent Hans Christian Andersen, *Lord of the Flies* author William Golding, Henry Miller, Lawrence Durrell, Evelyn Waugh, Virginia Woolf, and Florence Nightingale, have been entranced by their encounters with Greece. During the last century, hundreds of lesser known writers felt equally inspired to commit their experiences to print. For some, life in Greece has meant the fulfilment of non-intellectual aspirations. Nancy Spain explained that, when she was back in Britain, "I find myself thinking wistfully of the warm beaches where I might perhaps lie and recharge my run-down batteries" (1964:64). But for many visitors, Greece has represented a land of unparalleled cultural and historical significance. In the 1950s Monica Krippner sympathetically reported the sentiments of an Athenian she encountered at the Parthenon.

> You all come to my country for two days, maybe three. You see the temples, the ancient sites, all beautiful, all wonderful, all representing an age that has gone two thousand years . . . But of Greece, the real Greece of today, you learn almost nothing . . . And so Greece has become a kind of nostalgic retreat. (Krippner 1957:11-2)

For such travellers, the present was but a reflection of a more significant era. Greece was regarded as the cradle of civilization, the country to which Western culture owed its civic and moral virtues, as well as much of its art and drama. Many visitors were disappointed to find that the reflection in the mirror of antiquity was distorted by recent developments. But still, as Ian Brook believed, the past could "jostle" its way to the observer's attention. The "passion" for ancient Greece noted by Dilys Powell coloured visitors' expectations and perceptions.

In this book I show how travel writers described the people and monuments of Greece for consumption back home in Britain. I shall also be exploring the influences that lay behind these representations. In common with many other analysts of travel and tourism, I emphasise the subjectivity involved in viewing foreign locations. John Urry, for example, has argued that "one's sense of place is not simply given but is culturally constructed" (Urry 1990:2). Texts are now seen as integral to the tourist experience. Penny Travlou has suggested that guidebooks about Athens are "responsible for the construction of the image about the place that the tourists form in their minds" (2002:109). As a result, there has been a "recent upsurge of interest in travel writing" among scholars (Youngs 1997). There are currently two academic journals which specialize in this field (*Studies in Travel Writing* and *Journeys*), both of which were founded in the last ten years, and numerous other articles and books have been produced. A 2002 volume on travel writing in the *Cambridge Companions to Literature* series was described as the "first comprehensive introduction to the subject" (Hulme and Youngs 2002: cover).

The relationships between Britons and foreign cultures have also been of interest to those who study the ancient world. Classicists have increasingly felt it important to consider the history of their own discipline, as is demonstrated by the production of recent volumes reviewing so-called "reception studies" (Hardwick 2003; Martindale and Thomas 2006). There have been many studies of attitudes towards the ancient world. Such work has rarely been sweeping in its scope (Taplin 1989 is an exception), but has focused on certain areas—such as education (Stray 1998), drama (Hall 1999) and the cinema (Nisbet 2006; Winkler 2001)—or specific periods (Jenkyns 1980; Turner, F. 1981). The influence of Greece on art and architecture has been scrutinized by art historians (Watkin and Windsor Liscombe 2000) as well as classicists (Jenkyns 1991). A number of accounts covering the history of archaeology in Greece have been produced in recent years (Beard 2002; Fitton 1995; Shanks 1996), with the controversial careers of Lord Elgin, Schliemann at Mycenae, and Arthur Evans in Crete receiving detailed attention (MacGillivray 2001; St. Clair 1998; Traill 1995; Vrettos 1997).

The colourful exploits of nineteenth century visitors—including Lord Byron—have been recounted within a number of anthologies (Andrews 1979; Garrett 1994; Stoneman 1984; and Tomkinson 2002). There have also been attempts to situate these travellers within their historical context—the nineteenth century Western obsession with Greece—in works by Tsigakou (1981), Constantine (1984), Pemble (1987), and Angelomatis-Tsougarakis (1990). But travel writing about Greece in the twentieth century has been relatively neglected.[1] For example, in his 1991 history of travel to Greece, Robert Eisner admitted that he was able to examine only a selection of the hundreds of texts produced during the twentieth century (1991:1). Whilst such a lack of comprehensiveness is understandable, it obviously has serious repercussions. Ángel Quintana has observed that "our choice of texts will determine the conclusions we reach about the discourse we attempt to describe" (2001:177-8). This book is the first to analyse travel writing about Greece using all that was published in Britain during a given period. Rather than focusing merely on the big names who produced "quality" literature, I am, like John David Ragan in his study of French women travellers in Egypt, equally "interested in the ones with small budgets and lots of dreams" (2001:228).

In chapter one, I consider the nature and purpose of travel to Greece since the time of the Greek War of Independence. I identify the themes by which the—at that time relatively unknown—people of modern Greece were represented in travellers' texts of the nineteenth century. I also outline the exploration of ancient sites by archaeologists and others, and how these were then presented for public consumption. For example, the removal of later Turkish buildings left the Athenian Acropolis as a "frozen" aesthetic relic of the fifth century BC, a representation which has influenced travellers' writings right through to the present day. I consider in some detail the readership for the mid-twentieth century travel texts that form the focus of this book, since the period following the Second World War was a time of changing expectations and practices amongst tourists to Greece. 1940s travellers felt certain that there were potential readers for their books who shared their views and knowledge of the importance of ancient Greece and its material remains. As decades passed, however, travel writers were forced to realise that many of the increasing numbers of tourists to Greece had very different motives from those who had visited pre-war. In addition, changes to the British education system meant that, for many, classical Greece seemed a more distant and unfamiliar place than it had to earlier generations.

Whilst travel writing purports to record the thoughts of an individual, the author's attitudes have been affected by more than simply their own preferences, desires, prejudices or aptitudes: "travel experience involves mobility through an internal landscape which is sculptured by personal experience and cultural influences as well as journeying through space"

(Rojek 1997:53). Thus, in chapter two, I seek to identify the discourses which shaped British travellers' expectations of and responses towards Greece in the mid-twentieth century. During and immediately after the Second World War, British producers of news coverage and propaganda encouraged the public to view their wartime allies positively. Differences between the character and lifestyle of the British people and the Greeks were minimized. Connections were made between the qualities of the modern population and the ancient Greeks with whom the British were likely to be more familiar. Travel writers used these characteristics of bravery, nobility, democratic instincts, and continuity from the ancient world, in their portrayal of the modern Greeks that they encountered. In chapter two I also consider the nature of the British education system of the time, some popular textbooks on ancient history, and the widespread use of the classical style of art and architecture in the West. My argument is that British views of ancient Greece are central to understanding twentieth century perceptions of the modern country and its people. At the same time, however, it is clear that the Greek nationalist movement— dating back to at least the end of the eighteenth century—also contributed to the Western European idea of Greece as the heir of the ancient world. In the decades which followed the Second World War, Cold War politics demanded that the Greeks continue to be viewed as a democratic, friendly people, and this was reflected in travellers' writings.

My next two chapters comprise a detailed analysis of the representation within travel writing of two elements central to visiting Greece—the people and the ancient monuments. Chapter three focuses on major archaeological sites in mainland Greece (Athens, Bassae, Corinth, Delphi, Mycenae, Olympia, Sounion, Sparta) and the islands (Aegina, Crete).[2] In preparing this book, the description of these sites by each travel writer has been analysed with reference to a series of values and attributes. These include the aesthetics of the buildings and their surroundings; whether the viewer has been able to mentally reconstruct the site and transport him/herself to the past; if the site is said to confirm or deny information found in ancient texts; and any references given to ancient sources. Details of the development and application of this innovative method for analysing travel writing can be found in appendix C. As a result of this approach, I reveal in chapter three the common features in the representation of each site within travel accounts, as well as any changes which occurred across the period 1940-1974. Since, as I have argued, representations of foreign locations are not wholly dependent on what is there for travellers to see, I show how my findings relate to the other discourses I discussed in chapters one and two. The Athenian Acropolis for example was viewed as a monument to democracy, whereas the remains at Sparta were denigrated because of what was perceived as ancient folly. The dramatic nature of Delphi in travel accounts can be traced to its place in classical history as the scene of momentous events; the tranquillity of Olympia as related to the peace amongst states which accompanied the holding of the ancient games; and dark and brooding Mycenae as retaining the memory of bloody myths.

In chapter four the responses of travel writers to the people of Greece are analysed under three thematic headings. In forming my argument, I have, as with the sites and monuments, mapped the extent to which travel writers have ascribed various characteristics to the Greeks: generous or hospitable; brave or heroic; interested in politics or having democratic values; sociable or noisy; religious or superstitious; exhibiting a simple or pastoral way of life; and similarity or ethnic links to ancient people (see tables 5-7). I show that in some respects the Greeks were viewed as classical relics. They were frequently described by travel writers—directly and indirectly—as having the physical or behavioural characteristics which history textbooks assigned to their ancient forebears. This was sometimes deliberate, in order to emphasise Greek bravery and allegiance to democracy during the conflicts against fascism and then communism. But through their school and university education, travel writers and their readers were often more familiar with the ancient than the modern people, and the known was often employed to make sense of the unknown. The modern Greeks were regularly imagined to resemble figures from classical history, drama and mythology, or ancient sculpture. Travel writers also emphasised the timelessness of the Greek lifestyle, in particular the pastoral nature of the country. This was also a feature of anthropological writings of the same period, and stemmed from a desire to find the "primitive other" in Europe. The construction of the Greeks as the "other" sometimes had negative implications. Identifying certain characteristics as Turkish or "oriental" can be seen as part of a colonialist discourse in which Greeks were put in their place by the "superior" British.

The period following the Second World War was one of profound change for the people of both Britain and Greece. In some ways the dictatorship of the colonels in Athens (1967-74) represented a loss of innocence for British travellers in their relations with Greece, as well as scarring international diplomacy (and the lives of not a few Greeks). In a final chapter, I chart the history of travel writing from the mid-1970s onwards. Many of the earlier themes—the "primitive" Greeks, the importance of the monuments—persisted. Yet, by then, writers could no longer dismiss or ignore the changes which had been gradually taking place in their own potential readership, in the nature of the tourist experience, and in the people and infrastructure of Greece itself.

CHAPTER ONE

A HISTORY OF TRAVEL WRITING
ABOUT GREECE

(i) From Byron to the Second World War

In the two decades prior to the Greek War of Independence of 1821-30, travelling architects, diplomats and military men opened up for Western readers the archaeological sites and geography of Greece, then under Turkish dominion.[3] Lieutenant-Colonel William Martin Leake, for example, journeyed extensively in mainland Greece and the islands of Corfu and Kythera between 1800 and 1809. In the accounts he produced upon his return, he related how, with the writings of the second century AD Roman traveller Pausanias in hand, he had attempted to match remains on the ground to named ancient sites (Huxley 2001:39). William Gell's researches, which began in the same decade as those of Leake, resulted in what one modern commentator has dubbed "the first really practical travel guides since Pausanias" (Plouviez 2001:44). The architect C. R. Cockerell travelled in the region between 1810 and 1817, but his important volume on the temples at Bassae and Aegina did not appear until 1860 (Ferguson 2001:21). H. W. Inwood's 1819 surveys of the Athenian Acropolis resulted more immediately in the publication of *The Erechtheion at Athens* of 1827, as well as in his design for St Pancras Church in London (Ferguson 2001:33; see chapter two).

In 1810, during his first visit to Greece, Byron complained that "Athens is at present infested with English people" (Spencer, T. 1954:230). Certainly, the first three decades of the nineteenth century witnessed publication of a far greater number of travel accounts than had been the case in the 1700s (Wagstaff 2004:3). At least in part, this was due to the Napoleonic Wars effectively closing other possible European destinations to British travellers. The outbreak of the Greek war, in turn, ended what Hugh Ferguson has termed the "architectural phase of Greek archaeology" (2001:28), a time when gentlemen amateurs had made important discoveries through observation and small-scale excavation, as well as sometimes plundering the antiquities they recorded. The political landscape changed, and when research into ancient remains resumed, on an increasingly scientific basis, it would be overseen, if not actually conducted by, agencies of the Greek state. Intellectually, however, interpretations of Greek monuments and people within travel writing continued to be shaped and informed by discourses of British origin.

The struggle for independence received support from Philhellenes in the West due to a perceived debt: "there existed an urgent moral obligation for Europe to restore liberty to Greece as a kind of payment for the civilization which Hellas had once given to the world." (Spencer, T. 1954:vii) It was widely believed that in ancient Greece lay the origins of contemporary literature, architecture, political systems, and civic values. The work of Johann Winckelmann in the late eighteenth century popularised the notion that the ancient Greeks had achieved perfection in sculpture (Marchand 1996:7). But Philhellenes discovered that the Greeks in their present state did not always measure up to such elevated expectations. The French traveller F. C. H. L. Pouqueville noted in 1813 how the people of Kythera had changed since antiquity: "instead of Venus and the Graces, half wild Greek women" (Stoneman 1984:79). Shelley expressed his disgust to Trelawney in 1822.

> There is not a drop of the old Hellenic blood here. These are not the men to rekindle the old Greek fire; their souls are extinguished by traffic and superstition. (Hugo 1977:318)

With the end of hostilities and the escape from Ottoman control, Greece looked to the Western powers for political allies and governmental models. In turn, foreign observers regarded the Greeks as requiring development and Western tutelage, after centuries of being stifled by oriental lethargy. The progress of the Greeks had been held back by their Turkish masters: this was, according to Pouqueville, "a race of men who want only a proper system of government to be happy" (Pouqueville 1820:122). Greeks had degenerated on the surface—in learning and artistic output—but their fundamental character might have survived. George Cochrane (travelling 1834-6) was prepared to recognize their potential: "no people in the world are more capable and willing than the Greeks to learn and participate in the pleasures and refinements of modern civilization" (Andrews 1979:190).

For those nineteenth century travellers who were interested in costume, customs and beliefs, the "pre-modern" state of Greece was appealing. John Pentland Mahaffy advised readers in 1892 that they could "find in the hardy mountaineers of Greece one of the most unreformed societies, hardly yet affected by the great tide of sameness which is invading Europe" (Peckham 1999:166). Theodore Bent's stated purpose (1885:i) in visiting the islands of the Aegean was the recording of customs and beliefs—such as nereids (6ff), vampires (22), witches (187) and hobgoblins (174, 187)—which had by then disappeared from other parts of Greece. Some modern commentators have been too uncritical in their use of such writers for eyewitness information about Greece of the nineteenth century. Alan Sillitoe, for example, in using guidebooks to outline travellers' experiences, maintained that

> trawling through the various titles and editions enables one to confect a fair picture of what it was like to travel in the century up to the Great War of 1914. (1996:5)

Travel books are not without value as sources for the contemporary state of a country, but they are far from unproblematic. Tim Youngs, with reference to nineteenth century travelogues about Africa, has argued that

> too often they have been taken as straightforward evidence of their authors' claims without any critical attention being paid to the conditions of their production, their literary ideological constructions, or their reception. (1994:5)

As Youngs concluded,

> travellers do not simply record what they see. They travel with a purpose. They journey with preconceptions. They observe and write according to established models, having these in mind even when they wish to query or depart from them. (1994:209)

The contemporary travel writer Colin Thubron has said in an interview that

> someone else doing precisely the same journey may have encountered an utterly different reality, whatever we mean by this word reality. I think it's absurd for a travel writer to feel that he is really being objective, for there's no such thing. (Bassnett 1999:152)

Nineteenth century travellers, like their modern counterparts, inevitably referred to existing models, as well as their own beliefs and prejudices, when attempting to describe and interpret the people they encountered for their readers. In Greece, this often meant that writers sought the classical in the present. This served to establish a favourable identity for a people who had formerly been "merely" Turkish subjects. One form this took was the identification of physical similarities between modern Greeks and ancient individuals or artworks. The Reverend Henry Fanshawe Tozer, for example, chose to describe a sailor, Captain Constantine, as "Silenus in figure" and "Cyclops in face" (Tozer 1890:84). Some authors went further, positing that in the primitive lifestyle and traditions of Greek "peasants" could be found relics of ancient ways. In the 1880s, Bent claimed to have found all manner of continuities and similarities between ancient and modern: limb-shaped votive offerings (1885:229), goat bells (157), ploughs (48), the living conditions of shepherds (25), and beliefs about the afterlife (104). In matters of religion, Bent went so far as to say that "nowhere is one brought so closely face to face with the connecting links between heathendom and Christendom as one is in Greece" (Bent 1885:234). Tozer, more prosaically, claimed that the boots and cloak of Cretan men "seem to have come down from classical times", as he found them referred to by Galen and Aristophanes respectively (Tozer 1890:75).

Whilst Greece appeared very different from other nations—John Fuller reflected on arrival in the 1820s that "we were no longer in a civilized country" (Tomkinson 2002:69)—its status as European was redeemed by such classical links and heritage. But travellers also claimed to find the "Orient" in Greece, and this, too, had to be understood and explained. "Turkish" habits or practices were attributed to superficial and short-lived hangovers from the recent rulers, and were not considered to be fundamental features of Greek nature. Bent even posited that the veil worn by women he saw on Kythnos was a Homeric rather than a Turkish survival (Bent 1885:215). For many, Turkey and the East were synonymous with "mysticism, stasis, despotism, and stifling tribute" (Friedman 1992:839). For the Reverend Tozer, writing when Crete had not yet been freed from the Ottoman Empire, the island had been ruined by Turkish rule and insurrection. He reflected on Cretans he met who were in "great poverty" and concluded that "it must have required a large amount of misrule, neglect, and oppression to bring such a people to such a condition" (Tozer 1890:75). Such remarks also served a wider political agenda, helping to justify British rule and intervention in parts of the

Greek world. Cyprus, for example, remained under Ottoman control until 1878, when it was acquired by Britain. Faced with calls for union (*enosis*) with Greece, the colonial authorities downplayed the Greek nature of the island and its people, suggesting rather that this remained an outpost of the Orient that needed time under British rule to be "saved" (Severis 2000:192). Upon his arrival in Cyprus as part of the new regime, Lieutenant G. H. Lane reported back for *The Graphic* in London.

> The filthy unsanitary conditions of Larnaca and of other towns of Cyprus will soon disappear now that Western energy and skill have taken the place of eastern lassitude and ignorance. (Severis 2000:156)

Some writers criticized the Greeks for failing to better themselves. Captain T. A. B. Spratt complained that, even in relatively affluent areas of Crete, "the peasant takes no pains to render his habitation much better than that compartment which is appropriated to his beast" (Spratt 1865:179). However, more commonly, the efforts of the Greeks were viewed as contrasting favourably with the Eastern backwardness of the Turks. Rita Severis has pointed out that, in the 1870s illustrations of Louis Salvador, Turks are invariably "sitting on the ground, smoking a narghileh or seem to walk without direction", whereas the Greek figures are shown working (Severis 2000:140).

In visiting Greece, travellers often consciously set out to tread the soil touched by ancient feet. Terence Spencer pointed out in his classic study of literary Philhellenism that

> it is the associations of a place that primarily give it interest and beauty; not merely natural beauty, but also poetical associations, were the object of the sentimental traveller's search. (Spencer, T. 1954:266)

For some, it was enough merely to be at an ancient location, even if there was little to see. The Danish writer best known for his fairy tales, Hans Christian Andersen, approached the Peloponnese arguing that "each plot and patch has a value, an interest far greater than we sometimes feel for the richest landscape—because this was Greece!" (Andersen 1842:41) In Athens, Andersen urged his readers to consider that "every step one treads *is* on ground sacred with memories" (1842:54, original emphasis). Visible remains were perceived as providing a tangible link to the past. Bent was delighted to be able "to picture to ourselves the scenes of bygone ages" at the ruins on Delos (Bent 1885:113). At the beginning of the twentieth century Virginia Woolf felt that being in Greece enabled "the words of poets [to] begin to sing and embody themselves" (Morris 1993:205).

During the course of the nineteenth century there was progressively more of ancient Greece for travellers to view. A series of major excavation projects revealed the archaeological monuments which went on to become standard items on the itineraries of mid-twentieth century "cultural tourists". In Athens the Acropolis monuments began to be restored under Greek authority shortly after independence had been won. Most contemporary British travellers would have agreed with the strategy of sweeping away the structures dating from the Turkish period. Mary Beard has recently emphasised the extent to which "the present appearance of the site is largely the result of this campaign of clearance and excavation" (Beard 2002:102). The effects of the work of the early twentieth century were particularly dramatic on the Parthenon since it involved

> the re-erection of most of the missing sections of the long colonnades, which had the effect of joining up the east and west ends for the first time since the explosion of 1687. (Beard 2002:111)

Thus "the famous outline of the building, blazoned on postage stamps and tourist posters, was an invention of the 1920s" (Beard 2002:113). At the entrance to the Acropolis, the Temple of Athena Nike could not be seen until 1835, when, having been dismantled under the Ottomans, it was rebuilt. From the 1830s, design elements such as *entasis* (the curvature of the Parthenon's lines) were revealed as part of the first major studies of the Acropolis monuments since those of Stuart and Revett at the end of the eighteenth century (Tournikiotis 1996:45, 78), refinements which one traveller, Mrs Dawson Damer, demonstrated her knowledge of as early as 1839 (Damer 1842:28). Travellers of the early twentieth century were extremely interested in, and knowledgeable about, such minutiae of the buildings' construction. F. S. Burnell recorded the exact dimensions of the Parthenon, and the degree of *entasis* employed ("a maximum of .057 at a height of two-fifths of the column"; Burnell 1931:48). The focus for viewing the Acropolis had become its aesthetic value. It was "splendid as a work of art with its own crown of temples" (John Addington Symonds, 1898, quoted in Tsigakou 1981:119). In addition, for many visitors before the Second World War, the Acropolis not only possessed unsurpassed aesthetic qualities, but was symbolic of, and provided a link with, the culture which had produced it. St. John Ervine, for example, was astonished to find that it was more beautiful than I had imagined it to be, and, as I looked at it, I knew myself to be an Athenian, an unquenchable lover of Greece, knew what it was that sent Byron singing to Missolonghi to die, knew what it is that turns every civilised eye to this small, mountainous, almost barren country with the same conviction of satisfied spirit that the Moslem feels when he turns to Mecca, that moves the Christian when he sees the Cross. (Ervine 1936:90)

The excavation and reconstruction of the monuments of Athens from the 1830s onwards was not restricted to those on the Acropolis. Work was conducted on the Theatre of Dionysus from 1862 (MacKendrick 1962:284, 433), the location in which had been "recited all the great tragedies and comedies of the Athenian poets" (Hutton 1928:39). This restoration was so successful that John Addington Symonds wrote that it was "easy enough to dream ourselves into the belief that the ghosts of dead actors may once more glide across the stage" (Garrett 1994:5). However, it was not until the end of the 1930s that discoveries at the Temple of Hephaistus led archaeologists to restore to the building both its correct attribution (it was hitherto thought to have been dedicated to the hero Theseus), and modern equivalents of the vegetation with which it had originally been surrounded (MacKendrick 1962:240-1). The feature that primarily excited interest was its state of preservation. It was, as Edward Freeman observed, "the most perfect of existing Greek temples" (Freeman 1893:35). A similar (and lively) debate about the identity of the large temple in the vicinity of the Arch of Hadrian had appeared in the rival publications of James Stuart and Julien-David Le Roy at the end of the eighteenth century (Middleton 2004:20-3). This was finally confirmed as the Temple of Olympian Zeus once excavation had taken place in the 1880s (Middleton 2004:23). Excavations of the ancient Athenian marketplace (*agora*) have been conducted by the Americans from the 1930s through to the present, the interest centring upon evidence for politics and ordinary life rather than classical aesthetics (Mauzy 2006). The wholesale reconstruction of the Stoa of Attalus between 1953 and 1955 was one tangible result of this project for tourists.

Despite the variety of sites that were opened up for viewing, nineteenth century travel writers, like artists of the same period, often depicted Athens as dominated by the Acropolis, with other buildings reduced to insignificant smudges (Tsigakou 1991). Hans Christian Andersen commented that the Acropolis "stood like a gigantic throne high over all of the small houses" (1842:49). With the establishment of monarchical government, the new capital city saw changes wrought by King Otho's building projects, such as the royal palace (today the seat of parliament). The face of Athens was to change even more dramatically during the 1900s. Many of these developments were met with condescension by British writers of the mid-twentieth century, as we shall see in later chapters. As in Italy during the Grand Tour of the eighteenth century (Black 2003:160), the locals were thought not to sufficiently appreciate their heritage and to lack the aesthetic judgement to ensure that the modern city did not impinge upon the viewing of it. Edward Freeman professed to be "painfully struck by the glaring contrast of extreme antiquity and extreme newness" (1893:17). After thirty more years of change, St. John Ervine was left asking himself

> was this mean-looking shanty town, more wretched in looks than the worst shanty town I had seen in America, this incredibly nondescript, ugly and bungaloid hole, the entrance to the Parthenon? (Ervine 1936:90)

When Colonel Leake visited in 1805 the site of the ancient Olympic Games, it was as yet unexcavated. He thus found that "the scenery and topography are at present much more interesting than the ancient remains" (Hill Miller 1972:294-5). Olympia was excavated by the Germans from 1875, so that by the end of the century there was much more for visitors to see, including the Temple of Zeus. But writers continued to insist upon the importance of the surrounding landscape. The disruption to viewing caused by the archaeological work had temporarily led to disappointment, and thus reveals travellers' expectations: "instead of grass and flowers, and pure water, we found the classic spot defaced with great mounds of earth, and trodden bare of grass" (John Pentland Mahaffy, 1878, quoted in Garrett 1994:77). F. S. Burnell's description, in common with many of his contemporaries of the 1930s, emphasised the location, reporting an "atmosphere of tranquil, not to say melancholy, beauty" (Burnell 1931:185).

The site of ancient Delphi was excavated by the French from 1892, and by the mid-1940s the Temple of Apollo, the Treasury of the Athenians and the circular structure known as the Tholos had all been at least partially reconstructed (MacKendrick 1962:165-8). Nevertheless, for many in the first decades of the twentieth century it was the location of Delphi that captured the imagination—its "wild grandeur" and "uncanny quality" (Burnell 1931:161). This was the "centre of Greek religion" (Hutton 1928:145), where the riddles of the oracle had changed the course of Greek history. For H. V. Morton, the "haunted" atmosphere helped to explain the powerful psychological effect this location had in antiquity on those who came in search of answers to their dilemmas (Morton 1941:302).

Work at Corinth began under the Americans in 1896 and was still ongoing in the 1960s (MacKendrick 1962:413). This was a location of particular interest to those following in the footsteps of St. Paul, and F. S. Burnell found it easy to conjure up an image of the apostle within a bustling street scene (Burnell 1931:129-30). The Temple of Apollo at Bassae was known to Westerners from 1765, but the lack of a good access road until the late 1950s explains the relative neglect shown it by twentieth century travel writers. Ethel Smyth commented in the 1920s that "few people go there" (1927:97). Those who made the effort usually focused, as Mahaffy did in the 1870s and '80s, on the beauty of the setting and of the marble itself (Tomkinson 2002:116). On Aegina, the Temple of Aphaia had been denuded of its sculptures in 1811-2, so that subsequent travellers were left writing of "a great rectangular cluster of Doric columns supporting the broken architrave" (Hutton 1928:78). Nevertheless, the temple was much-visited, aided by the island's proximity to Athens. The site of ancient Athens' great rival, Sparta, also received a steady stream of visitors. It was, however, a deserted spot, with no modern settlement there until the end of the 1830s (Tsigakou 1991:103). Travellers found little of the ancient city either: "Sparta has disappeared. Not one stone is left upon another." (Hutton 1928:252) The Temple of Poseidon at Cape Sounion gained a reputation early-on for its aesthetics: "nothing can exceed the beauty of this spot", commented William Gell towards the beginning of the nineteenth century (Hill Miller 1972:92). By the time Virginia Woolf visited in 1932 it could be described simply as "the Temple on a cliff" (Morris 1993:219). For Morton, also writing in the 1930s, Sounion's credentials as the perfect ruin were completed by Lord Byron having inscribed his name into the stone, making it "all too good to be true" (Morton 1941:317).

The lion gate at Mycenae was a sight well-known to travellers of the early nineteenth century. Whilst clearance work at the gate was undertaken by the newly formed Greek Archaeological Society in 1841 (Gere 2006:59), it was not until the 1870s that the imaginative as well as physical landscape of Mycenae was transformed by Heinrich Schliemann's excavations. With Schliemann's revelation that he had discovered the last resting-place of Agamemnon, protagonist of Homer's Trojan War, the site's connection to myth and legend gained in immediacy. When Virginia Woolf visited in 1906 she found "the taste of

Homer in my mouth" (Morris 1993:205). The work of archaeologist Christos Tsountas late in the nineteenth century had revealed a palace atop the Mycenaean acropolis, and in the 1950s a second grave circle was added to that discovered by Schliemann (Gere 2006:96, 157). By that time, writers were conscious of earlier errors: Schliemann and his wife had been "wrong in imagining that their finds were from the period of Agamemnon" (Anderson 1964:148). But Schliemann's work left an enduring impression on the way the site was scripted. Whilst Ethel Smyth in the 1920s described the landscape positively as "gorgeous" (Smyth 1927:59), as the twentieth century wore on, the idea that a visit to Mycenae inspired dread and awe became commonplace within travel literature. The shadow of the family of Atreus, familiar from ancient tragedy, continued to loom over the present remains.

This list of major excavated sites on the tourist trail received an addition from 1900 in the form of Sir Arthur Evans' Knossos on Crete. T. A. B. Spratt had informed nineteenth century readers that "the only vestiges of Gnossos [sic] at the present time are some scattered foundations and a few detached masses of masonry of the Roman time" (Spratt 1865:59). As early as 1901 Evans had begun to restore parts of the palace of King Minos he was uncovering, at first to meet conservation concerns but moving on to more wholesale "reconstitutions" (as he called them) in the 1920s, using concrete (Fitton 1995:128-30). From the beginning, what awaited the visitor was controversial, recently characterized by Lesley Fitton as a "beguiling mixture of the real and the restored" (Fitton 1995:116). Burnell, however, found Knossos "pregnant with interest and that rather indefinable quality which one calls 'atmosphere'" (Burnell 1931:20). Evelyn Waugh felt "oppressive wickedness" there.

> I do not think that it can be only imagination and the recollection of a
> bloodthirsty mythology which makes something fearful and malignant of
> the cramped galleries and stunted alleys, these colonnades of inverted,
> conical pillars, these rooms that are mere blind passages at the end of
> sunless staircases. (Waugh 1930:137)

Travel writers of the early twentieth century could assume that readers shared their appreciation of the importance of Greece's material heritage.

> We have all been familiar with pictures of the Acropolis and the Parthenon
> since we were children. We have seen them in books, in the vicar's study,

in steamship offices; and we have received them on postcards from every
friend who has gone on a Hellenic cruise. (Morton 1941:280)

At Marathon, Morton was emphatic that "every intelligent traveller in
Greece wants to see the site of the famous battle" (Morton 1941:313). The
knowledge of ancient Greece which travellers carried with them certainly
affected their expectations and perceptions of what they saw. Eric Gifford
attempted to distance himself from this process: "I myself was spared a
Classical education. I had few fixed illusions, therefore, on which to build
my mental picture of Athens." (Gifford 1939:13) For many others,
however, this was "the only fairyland of our youth that the years had not
stolen away" (Hutton 1928:80). Travellers often desired a Grecian
experience in which they could commune with the spirits of the ancients,
admire their surviving monuments, and remain unaffected and untouched
by modernity. The effects and experiences of the First World War
provided further motivation for travelling and living abroad in a spirit of
escapism.

The Greeks were regularly represented as pre-modern in their lifestyle,
which assisted those who wished to journey in time as well as space in
Greece. Greek country-people were almost invariably—and casually—
described as "peasants". As in the nineteenth century, locals had classical
comparisons foist upon them. Robert Byron found a monk in Athos "of
extraordinary resemblance, both in feature and expression, to the well-
known bust of [the Athenian statesman] Pericles" (Byron 1928:71).
Morton saw shepherds who "might have stepped from an ancient frieze or
from a Greek vase" (Morton 1941:314). Patterns of behaviour had also
apparently survived across the centuries. F. S. Burnell found that
"Athenians of today are no less ready than of old to indulge in political
experiments", and further suggested that the bravery shown by Greeks in
their struggles against the Turks showed a link between ancient and
modern (Burnell 1931:16, 97). William Miller went so far as to argue that
"the average Greek of classical times must have had most of the
characteristics of the modern Hellenes" (Miller, W. 1905:3). The modern
people were regarded as the preservers of ancient traditions and beliefs.

The superstitions of the Greek peasant are entirely classical. The gods, the
nymphs, and the satyrs of yesterday have become the ogres and bogies of
today. (Morton 1936:299)

Upon hearing of the Euboian funeral custom of placing money in the deceased's hands, Miller chose to consider this a "curious survival of the obol to serve as passage-money across the Styx" (Miller, W. 1905:96).

The positive qualities of the Greek race were regularly rehearsed within early twentieth century travel writing, in particular their politeness and hospitality. Olive Murray Chapman was evidently delighted to report that "in no other country, with the exception possibly of Iceland, have I met with greater courtesy and kindness than that I experienced among the Cypriots" (Chapman 1937:127). For Morton, this too could be traced to antiquity.

> It is among the common people of Greece, among the fishermen, the shepherds, the hillmen, and the peasants, that one seems to catch the echo of the hospitality of the Homeric age and the simplicity of Theocritus. (Morton 1941:310)

Travel writers of the first decades of the twentieth century experienced a diluted version of the generosity which their predecessors had usually demanded. Nineteenth century visitors—despite their evident wealth—had often travelled across Greece supported by gifts of accommodation and sustenance. Captain Spratt was unusual, in that he preferred to pitch his tent, weather permitting (Spratt 1865:86). Bent eventually found the attention he received wearisome, "after months of travel amongst hospitable, but occasionally rather boring, families, whose idea of hospitality was never to leave us alone, for fear we should be dull" (Bent 1885:126). By the beginning of the 1900s this was changing, with payment both expected and subject to market forces: "I can only remember one outrageous attempt at extortion, and that at a place spoilt by tourists" (Miller, W. 1905:14).

At the same time, if writers chose to emphasise Turkish elements, this could be described as an "oriental"—rather than a classical—country. Morton noted the string of beads which he called "the rosary of the Orient", and "the blue beads which Moslems believe to be a charm against the evil eye" (Morton 1941:280). Miller observed that, since there was so little to be seen in Athens of the Byzantine, Frankish or Turkish periods, "the traces of these intermediate ages must be sought in the manners and customs of the Athenians rather than in the scanty monuments of Latin and Turkish domination" (Miller, W. 1905:183). Such arguments emphasising the existence of non-Greek elements were most prevalent with reference to the population of Cyprus. This mirrored the ongoing efforts of British officials to place distance between their subjects and mainland Greeks, and was also aided by contemporary archaeologists who posited a distinct culture for Cypriots in antiquity (Severis 2000:206). Gifford noted that

> English [*sic*] officials are largely pro-Turk. For some reason it is considered chic to prefer the Turks to the Greeks. Also there is the good political reason that the Greeks are always agitating to be united to Greece, whereas the Turks prefer the *status quo*. (Gifford 1939:38)

Chapman found a "picturesque Eastern atmosphere so marked throughout the island" (Chapman 1937:58-9). She described even wholly Greek villages as "very Eastern-looking with their flat roofs, [and] sun-baked walls of mud and straw" (Chapman 1937:58). Following the Second World War, the idea of a Turkish legacy had not entirely faded from the minds of travellers to the Greek world, but its effects were usually to be seen in more subtle forms than in descriptions of houses, dress or traditions. Instead, it was used to account for undesirable or odd behaviour—dishonesty and lack of timekeeping, for example—thus rescuing other essential Greek characteristics as Western and/or ancient. An earlier user of this argument was Eric Gifford, when he attributed sharp practice to the Turkish occupation.

> It was a case of cheating the conquerors. In those days, the Cypriot made the most of what little he had, against the ever present time when it might be snatched by some rapacious pasha. (Gifford 1939:19)

Travel writing is, as I have suggested, far from an uncomplicated record of places and people. It is subject to a series of, often, competing and contradictory concerns and ideas. As Sara Mills has pointed out, examples of the genre

> cannot be analysed as if the texts originated from one determining factor, such as the author, "reality", imperialism or femininity, but rather that the texts are produced in the interaction and clashing of a variety of constraining factors. (Mills 1991:68-9)

Travel writers often desperately wanted to find "their" ancient Greeks inhabiting the Greece of the present. Virginia Woolf, for example, tried to be positive. In 1906 she emphasised that "most of the poor people who are not inn keepers, seemed courteous and cheerful" (Morris 1993:203). But she nevertheless found her conceptions of Greekness challenged.

The people of Athens are, of course, no more Athenians than I am. They
do not understand the Greek of the age of Pericles—when I speak it. Nor
are their features more classic than their speech. (Morris 1993:212-3)

To date, however, travel writing about Greece has been little-used as a
source for understanding attitudes towards antiquity in the twentieth
century. In chapter two I chart some of the influences I have so far merely
touched upon—classical education, art, architecture and literature—which
shaped the writings of travellers. First, in the remainder of this chapter, I
look at travel writers, their aims and literary output, from the core period
of this study—the mid-twentieth century.

(ii) From 1940 to the Fall of the Colonels (1974)

It can be difficult to produce a definition for "travel writing" which can
comfortably accommodate all of the works of literature that we might wish
to attach to it. "Non-fiction with a foreign setting" is a beginning, but, as
Mark Cocker has pointed out, this would encompass guidebooks as well as
anthropological studies (Cocker 1992:104, 113-4). A guidebook is
addressed to those planning to follow the writer to a location, its principal
purpose being to impart factual information to the traveller. Hence, Giles
Barber has defined a guidebook as a "usually pocket size work which the
traveller is expected to take with him [*sic*] and consult on the spot"
(Barber, G. 1999:94). Travel writing may, rather, be said to be *primarily*
an evocation of a place for those who do not intend to go themselves, or
who want a reminder or comparison to their own experiences. In practice,
though, this division becomes indistinct, since travel writing often contains
passages of history or information, and it is often physically carried by
travellers as a form of guide. In addition, the production of a guidebook is
not exempt from the process of selection, prioritization and ordering made
by an author or authors. But whereas in a guidebook it is intended that the
reader is the hero—*we* will have the experiences, in the present tense—
travel writing foregrounds the *author* as the protagonist. Thus, in this book
I have taken "travel writing" to mean a first-person narrative of an author's
journey to a specific foreign location.

Nevertheless, as in earlier times, travel writing about Greece in the
three decades following the Second World War came in various forms and
was published for a variety of reasons. During the war Greece had, as the
International Labour Office recognized in 1947, "suffered more severely
than any other allied country except the Soviet Union" (Woodhouse
1976:161). Hilda Hughes' 1944 edited volume was published in aid of the

Greek Red Cross (1944:177ff), and the inclusion of details of the suffering caused by the Axis occupation was designed to give readers the opportunity to identify with the modern Greeks. As early as 1941, Dilys Powell had been exhorting British readers to *Remember Greece* as the occupation commenced, and she outlined in her travel book the notable efforts of the Greek military from 1939 onwards. Following the end of the war, British agents who had worked with the resistance returned to Greece and published their views of what had happened to the country and its people in the years since their departure. Amongst these were Xan Fielding's *The Stronghold: An Account of the Four Seasons in the White Mountains of Crete* (1953) and Patrick Leigh Fermor's more famous two volumes, *Mani: Travels in the Southern Peloponnese* (1958), and *Roumeli: Travels in Northern Greece* (1966).

Writers of the post-war period expressed a variety of reasons for their travels. Penelope Tremayne and Evan John recorded medical missions they had undertaken—respectively, as a Red Cross nurse in Cyprus, and to bring relief supplies to earthquake-stricken Ithaca (Tremayne 1958; John 1954). Stanley Evans, Chancellor of Southwark Cathedral, was visiting Greece en route to the Holy Land as part of an organised pilgrimage (Evans 1965). Clara Vyvyan's visit began as a quest for wild flowers, whilst Paul Hogarth's drawings were a commentary on politics in Greece and the role of the British (Vyvyan 1955:25; Hogarth 1953:1, 22, 25, 29). Since the style and focus of these books varied, so, by extension, did their projected readership. Several writers sought to provide an informative and authoritative account of their subject. As a result of his visit to the disaster zone of the Ionian Islands, John was able to "write the first full-length story of the effect which the earthquake had on the survivors" (John 1954: jacket). W. A. Wigram believed that "for some time to come, visitors to Greece are likely to rely on the 'Cruising ship' for their means of travel" and he therefore produced a book, "the fruit of some years of experience in that sort of travel, in the hope that it will enable folk to understand what they have come a long way to see" (Wigram 1947:11). Likewise, Robert Liddell's *The Morea* was publicized as being useful to the traveller on the ground.

> Too various and entertaining to be called a guide-book, this is in fact an ideal handbook for the region, exploring not only the best known sites . . . but many lesser places little known and seldom visited. (Liddell 1958: jacket)

Other travellers in search of knowledge about Greece—the
professional anthropologists—have found useful records of beliefs,
traditions and ways of life within some of the travel writing produced
since the 1940s. Ernestine Friedl (1962:75, 109-10) cited as containing
"valuable descriptions of the land and the people" the travel books of
Lawrence Durrell, Kevin Andrews (1959), Henry Miller (1942), and C. P.
Lee (1957). Durrell, for example, had appended "A Short Calendar of
Flowers and Saints for Rhodes" and "Peasant Remedies" to his *Reflections
on a Marine Venus* (Durrell, L. 1953:185ff). Juliet du Boulay also
acknowledged the assistance of Kevin Andrews with her book *Portrait of
a Greek Mountain Village* (1974: preface). The jacket of his *Flight of
Icarus* (1959) had emphasised its anthropological value: he had
"journeyed among regions and populations of Greece with which outsiders
do not, as a rule, have the temerity to get themselves involved."

As Malcolm Crick has pointed out, the anthropologist and the traveller
have similar goals and methodologies: "both travel to collect and
expropriate what they value from the other and then tell of their journeys"
(Crick 1995:210). Some anthropologists were still publishing the fruits of
their research in Greece long after they had ceased to be "in the field".
Renée Hirschon's 1989 volume relied on her residence in Piraeus during
the early 1970s (1989:xviii), and du Boulay was writing about North
Euboea in 1991 from information she had gathered between 1966 and
1973 (1991:38). Other anthropologists' research emerged more swiftly in
book form alongside the work of their contemporaries as travel writers.
Ernestine Friedl's main report, for example, appeared in 1962, the year
after she had concluded her fieldwork (Friedl 1962:ix, xi). Greece was at
that time regarded as a new and unusual region for anthropological work.
John Campbell later reflected that "the prospect of working in a country
where none had gone before seemed to me an attractive challenge"
(1992:149). Invariably the anthropologists of that generation chose to
centre their work on rural communities. Whereas the "earliest research
carried out by a British social anthropologist in Greece" was that of
Campbell in 1954-5 (Campbell 1992:148), Hirschon's 1989 book could be
described by Michael Herzfeld as "the first full ethnography of an *urban*
setting in Greece" (Hirschon 1989:xiii, my emphasis). Roger Just admitted
that as late as the 1970s he "had wanted to study a traditional village, and
had gone to some lengths to find one" (Just 2000:5). As a result, Greece
emerged in anthropological studies as a series of primitive, isolated and
unchanging communities. Some anthropologists propounded
"survivalism", the idea that "certain institutions or customs are very

ancient and can be traced in their unchangingness back to as long ago as possible" (Davis 1977:251; see chapter two). One of the most extensive studies of survivalism in the Mediterranean was produced by Richard and Eva Blum, who devoted about one-third of their book to a comparison of their fieldwork findings with the beliefs of *ancient* Greeks. As a result they claimed to have discovered "impressive evidence of continuity in Greek thought with reference to crisis and mystery" (Blum and Blum 1970:2).[4] Only rarely can it be shown that travel writers were directly influenced by anthropological sources. Joseph Braddock admitted to having consulted the work of Blum and Blum (on health and healing), and Leslie Finer recommended Ernestine Friedl's *Vasilika* (Braddock 1970:195; Finer 1964:253). Whilst the writings of anthropologists in Greece do not form the focus of this book, some of their representations of its people are similar to those found within travel writing of the same period, as we shall see in chapter four.

Indeed, the focus for many travel writers was the present inhabitants of the country rather than the ancient sites. Patrick Anderson explained that he was

> more interested in what *ouzo* looked like, and tasted like, than in the acoustics of an ancient theatre or the location of a shrine . . . Above all, Greece attracted me because the people were said to be friendly and talkative, and I hoped to sit at cafés with them and hear what they had to say. (Anderson 1958:16-7)

Joseph Braddock's publisher sought to promote the idea that his book "conveys with a poet's insight the basic contentment and uncomplicated values of the people, their friendliness and humanity" (1967: jacket). But many strove to make their literary encounters with the Greeks primarily entertaining rather than offering serious analysis of national character and lifestyle. Xan Fielding's stated aim in producing his book on the White Mountains of Crete was not the proper anthropological work that he believed the area deserved, but merely "the account of a more or less carefree year spent among people who seem to fit so perfectly into their startling surroundings" (Fielding 1953:xvi). Hazel Thurston explicitly made "no pretence of being seriously informative" (Thurston 1960: jacket).

Readers were advised that some travel books would reveal as much about the character of the writer as the subject country. According to his publisher, David Dodge produced a book of "adventures".

From it you will learn a lot about Europe, money, people, and how to treat
your wife, and how not, what *les jeunes filles* are like, and above all, what
a person this Mr Dodge is. (1955: jacket)

Potential readers of Gerald Durrell's *My Family and Other Animals* were
advised that it was "a matter of personal taste whether one most enjoys the
family, with its many eccentric hangers-on", or the stories about the
animals (Durrell, G. 1959: cover). Some of the books, like Durrell's, I
have classified as travel writing might rather be considered autobiography
or memoir. The title of Compton Mackenzie's 1960 work—*Greece in My
Life*—reflects its focus on the author's long relationship with the country
and its people (including his career as a military intelligence officer during
the First World War). Joice NanKivell Loch's *A Fringe of Blue* (1968) is
even subtitled *An Autobiography*. However, in both of these books the
writers devote substantial sections to their travels in Greece and their
observations of the people they encountered. Consequently, the potential
reader was advised that

> the life of the peasant community into which they were swept is vividly
> portrayed by Mrs Loch, with all its customs, superstitions and intrigues,
> and many unforgettable characters who became fast friends. (Loch 1968:
> jacket)

Gerald Durrell opened his book with "this is the story of a five-year
sojourn that I and my family made on the Greek island of Corfu" (1959:9).
The works by Durrell, Loch and Mackenzie are examples of an important
sub-genre of travel writing about Greece—the memoir of an extended stay
(Wills 2005a). Others published during the mid-twentieth century period
include those by Bull (1967), Carroll (1965), Chamberlain (1965), Clift
(1958 and 1959), Lawrence Durrell (1945, 1953 and 1957), Matthews
(1971), Powell (1957), and Travis (1970). These are accounts produced by
those who were initially outsiders, but who became "stationary travellers".
Some were women who, having married Greeks, were settling in their
husbands' native land. Others went in search of an improved quality of
life. In the 1960s Joseph Braddock sought out the Australian-born Kester
Berwick, who explained his reasons for living on Lesbos.

> Do you think I regret leaving London, getting out of the rat-race? Here I
> have what I most want—not much money—but beauty, peace of mind,
> leisure to write as I feel like it. (Braddock 1967:52)[5]

After years of devastating war, many writers were in search of escape, or meaning. Lawrence Durrell, in his account of his residency on Corfu, maintained that "other countries may offer you discoveries in manners or lore or landscape; Greece offers you something harder—the discovery of yourself" (1945:11). Much later, Willy Russell captured this attitude in his play (and subsequent film) *Shirley Valentine*, in which the eponymous heroine refuses to return to Britain at the end of her holiday because she had "fallen in love with the idea of livin'" (Russell 1988:33).

John Sykes decided against buying a house and living in Greece, as he felt it would be dishonest to pretend that he could ever be more than an outsider (1965:156-7). In contrast, many who became residents claimed to have greater insight than other travel writers and thus to be able to portray the "real Greece". There was criticism of non-residents' idealized representation of the Greek people and their way of life. Lawrence Durrell in particular complained of "sentimental" writing about peasants (1945:36). As a woman who had lived in Kalamata for ten years as the wife of a Greek, Sheelagh Kanelli was scathing about "fly-by-nights who bask on a sunny island for a few months and go home saying how wonderful Greece is" (1965:30). Some eschewed frivolous stories about Greeks and claimed their work as a manifesto for an alternative way of living. Charmian Clift's *Peel me a Lotus* was trumpeted as not "merely another family chronicle of life among the peasants", but rather "a passionate exploration of the pervasive twentieth-century problem of nomadism" (1959: jacket).

Many of the travel books I have considered in this study, particularly those by authors who were residents, have only a portion of Greece as their subject. Some writers decided to focus on a distinct part of the mainland (Forbes-Boyd 1965, 1970; Leigh Fermor 1958, 1966; Liddell 1954, 1958, 1965). Freya Stark's 1956 *The Lycian Shore* was primarily concerned with the coast of Turkey, but has early chapters on the Greek islands of Chios, Samos, Patmos, and Calymnos. David Dodge was likewise *Talking Turkey* (1955), but his drive across Europe took in Greece. Goran Schildt (1953) began his sail across the Mediterranean from northern Italy, but the majority of his published account was devoted to Greece (pp.82-293, of a total of 315). Cyprus has been included in my definition of Greece, in part because the representation of Greek political attitudes within travel writing cannot be analysed without reference to the issue of *enosis* (see chapters two and four). The Greeks of that island were in many respects portrayed identically to those of the mainland. When they were viewed differently, this too proves illuminating, as we have seen in travel writing of the first decades of the twentieth century.

Travellers in Greece are revealed through their writings to have had a variety of backgrounds. I have not dismissed from my consideration those few non-native authors whose work was published in Britain. The list of ninety-two books of the mid-twentieth century which forms appendices A and B therefore includes accounts by Australians (Charmian Clift [1958, 1959] and Colin Simpson [1969]), Americans (Henry Miller [1942], Emily Kimbrough [1957, 1965], Herbert Kubly [1970] and John Pierson [1973]), and by a Swedish-Finn (Goran Schildt [1953]). The issuing of these texts indicates faith on the part of publishers of their attractiveness to the British market, either because the authors agreed with or challenged visions of Greece commonly held in this country. I have also included a text in which the writer, Barbara Whelpton, assumed a persona—that of Anna, a 21-year-old travelling to Greece for the first time—in order to appeal to a young audience (Whelpton 1954). Whelpton's writing was, however, based on real travel experiences, as her other work attests (Whelpton and Whelpton 1961). Classical references within travel writing reveal that authors often possessed considerable knowledge of ancient history and literature, and that they expected much the same from their readers. Patrick Anderson encountered a smell like that of the wound of Philoctetes, and Robert Liddell found a guide who walked "as proudly as the shade of Achilles in the fields of asphodel" (Anderson 1958:107; Liddell 1965:117). Both Peter Bull and S. F. A. Coles professed to having had only a limited formal classical education (Bull 1967:2-3; Coles 1965:27), yet Coles referred to relatively minor ancient writers such as Menander and Aulus Gellius (Coles 1965:73, 74). Some authors became famous for their travel writing (Leigh Fermor), or their novels (Lawrence Durrell), and hence their books concerning Greece have had a number of reprintings over several decades. Most of the books listed in my appendices were not republished, however. *Cider with Rosie* author Laurie Lee's slim volume about his filming in Cyprus (Lee and Keene 1947) rapidly became a rarity, and even Henry Miller's celebrated *Colossus of Maroussi* has in recent times fallen out of print.

Of the travel books I have used, sixty-five were written by men, twenty-three by women, and a further four by male and female co-authors (see appendix A). There have been a number of studies (e.g. Blunt 1994; Frawley 1994; Lawrence 1994; and Mills 1991) examining the effects of gender on the content and structure of travel writing. It has, for example, been argued that in accounts by women of the nineteenth century "there is a clear assertion of femininity, either through attention to details of clothing, accounts of domestic life, or the inclusion of romantic episodes" (Bassnett 2002:239). It is, however, important to recognize that "the sheer diversity of women's travel writing resists simple classification" (Bassnett 2002:239). Since I have studied all travel books about Greece published in Britain between 1940 and 1974, I have not selected my sources on the basis of gender. I have also discerned no difference in the nature of accounts produced by men and women. The tales of "domestic drama", for example, related by those who were resident in Greece, can be found in writing by both sexes (e.g. Clift 1958:123ff; Travis 1970:133ff).

As I have already suggested, some writers assumed the existence of a shared (classical) culture with their readers, and an appreciation of the importance and value of the ancient world. To understand Ashley Smith's explanation of his feelings as he viewed the Acropolis clearly required prior knowledge about ancient authors and artists.

> The whole of Greece is here. The beauty of its past. Those figures who will never die: Thucydides, Homer, Sappho, Phidias, Euripides, Praxitiles. (Smith, A. 1948:184)

Here Smith (like others of his time) was essentially adopting the persona of the nineteenth century "gentleman traveller", as described by Caren Kaplan: "an introspective observer, literate, acquainted with ideas of the arts and culture, and, above all, a humanist" (1996:50). Readers of such passages were not learning anew, but were having their existing values affirmed. In Robert Liddell's mind, "everyone knows" the story of Oedipus, and "no educated person (until he is very well used to it) can pass through the railway station on the north, and read the name Thebes quite unmoved" (Liddell 1965:6, 7). In reaction to such assumptions, some writers reassured their readers that less stringent demands or qualifications were required of them. Peter Bull's readers "need have no fear that he has delved deep into the mythology or history of Greece" (1967: jacket), and the author made efforts to explain all references he made (e.g. to Icarus: Bull 1967:66).

Bull also expressed anxiety about the possible effects of his writings. In the "Postscript" to his book he explained his dilemma about naming his island hideaway (Paxos, in fact).

On the one hand, one is dying to show off one's perception and cleverness and, on the other, one is trying to prevent other persons going there. The moment dear witty lamented Nancy Spain mentioned the island of Sciathos in *The News of the Woggers* [*sic*] the price of land rocketed up and a great many people made a bee-line for it on their next holiday, having never previously heard of the place. It is obvious to me that the newspaper public is avid for suggestions and will react as strongly to an article as they do to an effective advertising campaign. (Bull 1967:161)

Many writers were aware that writing about "their" island, or the Greek way of life in general, threatened to spoil what they had discovered. This is, of course, a trope familiar to analysts of tourism, sometimes referred to as a "middle-class anxiety" (Urry 1990:42). But it was a particularly acute concern for those, like Bull, who were resident in Greece, rather than simply there occasionally on holiday. The journalist Nancy Spain, referred to by Bull, had observed that "the whole world seemed to be on a Greek-island-buying jag", but nevertheless decided to have a house built for herself on Skiathos (Spain 1964:145). In his account published a year later than that of Spain, Michael Carroll, who himself settled on Skopelos, declared that Skiathos was "already in danger of becoming that sad creature of illusion, a tourist island" (Carroll 1965:121).

Some books were apparently aimed at those who were staying at home in Britain. Louis Golding's book was said to be "a holiday by itself" (1955: jacket). Robert Bell's publisher assured readers that "when you come to the end of this volume you, too, will feel that you have made the journey, but in the comfort of your arm-chair" (1961:15). But writing might also be designed to encourage travel. Robert Liddell's *Aegean Greece* would "lure many to follow his example" (1954: jacket). In the 1960s package holidays were still the exception rather than the rule, and so many travel writers tried to give practical information as well as their personal impressions. Bell's primary aim in writing his book was, in fact, to help and inform those who intended to follow in his tyre-tracks, *By Road to Greece*: "I have endeavoured to answer all the questions which you may ask about the journey to Greece and what happens when you get there" (1961:21). Robert Liddell's second book, on *The Morea*, was envisaged as "a most helpful and agreeable travelling companion" (1958: jacket).

By the early 1970s tourism to Greece was more "mass" than it had been thirty years before. Over the previous two decades the Greek government had attempted to encourage this aspect of the country's economy through improvements to infrastructure and the establishment of the Greek Tourist Organization (GTO). By the 1960s tourists were coming in much larger numbers. In 1938 Greece had just 90,000 visitors (Close 2002:55). By 1960, when the first Greek tourism office opened in London, this had risen to 399,000, then to 1.6 million by the end of the decade (Gibbons and Fish 1990:474; Bray and Raitz 2001:82). Corfu, for example, had become a place where "*To saison* (the season) has begun to be spoken of" (Tennant 2002:77). At first, as Eleana Yalouri has explained, the GTO envisaged Greeks as having "the role of hosts who also had the responsibility to introduce the foreign pilgrims to both past and present Hellenism" (Yalouri 2001:128). This seemed appropriate because

> until the 1950s tourism to Greece had been mainly "cultural", consisting of "travellers" continuing, in a way, the tradition of the eighteenth and nineteenth centuries. Their voyages to Greece were more like "pilgrimages", paying homage to the countries that "gave birth to civilization". (Yalouri 2001:130)

However, the period from 1940 until the early 1970s saw changes not merely to the number of tourists but in their expectations and knowledge of Greece. The "sun, sea and sand" motive became increasingly prevalent. By the time the sociologist Selanniemi studied Finnish tourists to Greece in the 1990s, a polarisation in habits and expectations could be seen. Those who went to Athens did so "because of its cultural and historic distinctiveness", whilst Rhodes as a choice of destination was "in many ways interchangeable with other resorts in 'the south'" (Meethan 2001:76). To use recent sociological terminology, the "tourist gaze" had changed. For "romantic" tourists, the ideal experience consisted of "solitude, privacy and a personal, semi-spiritual relationship with the object of their gaze" (Urry 1990:45). But for increasing numbers of tourists, the focus of their travel would involve a "collective" experience, with the presence of (large numbers of) other people being seen as desirable (Urry 1990:45-6; Urry 1995:191). On Rhodes, for example, the tourists Selanniemi observed "slept late, spent a great deal of time on the beach, and at night, often ended up partying until the early hours of the following morning" (the latter, by definition, a group activity; Meethan 2001:76). Even for those who still travelled to Greece for the cultural sights, the nature of the experience had changed somewhat during the post-war period. Rather than leading travellers on a sacred journey, the Greek tourist guides of the 1990s characterized their charges as saying "It is Tuesday, so we are in Athens" (Yalouri 2001:130). Developments in the

British education system and the esteem in which the classical world was held meant that, increasingly from the 1960s onwards, tourists viewed ancient sites with less time and less knowledge. Writers and publishers of travel literature underwent a slow realisation that their readers might require more explanation of the importance of the monuments of Greece than those of earlier decades and generations had needed.

Shortly after the end of the Second World War, Osbert Lancaster's stated aims for his book were as follows.

> To provide some general account of the present appearance and condition of Greece that may perhaps prove of use to that small minority who are likely in future to receive the necessary passports, visas, priorities, travel-permits and foreign exchange enabling them to leave these shores, to awaken a not-too-painful nostalgia in those who have visited the country in the past, and to provide some slight entertainment and instruction to the vast majority who lack the memories of the latter and entertain no hopes of immediate inclusion in the narrow ranks of the former. (1947:8)

For a time, writers viewed travel to Greece as the preserve of a relatively privileged few. Not merely those who, as Lancaster suggests, possessed the tenacity to negotiate complicated bureaucracy, but those with the learning and culture to fully appreciate that ancient country and its modern incarnation. The period from the 1950s to the early 1970s witnessed a democratization of travel, but, as we shall see, literary interpretations of the people and monuments of Greece were not so rapidly transformed.

CHAPTER TWO

THE BRITISH AND THE GREEKS

Penny Travlou, in her recent analysis of guidebooks, stresses that "the people who created the symbolic images of Athens are the nineteenth century travellers to Greece" (2002:110). As I have shown in the previous chapter, post-1940 travel writers certainly had literary models stretching back into the nineteenth century for their views of Greece, its people and monuments. However, there were three discourses of the twentieth century which were particularly important in shaping writing of the period, and these form the subject of this chapter. The British system of formal education, which often included a considerable slice of learning about ancient history and literature, affected perceptions of Greece. During and after the Second World War, British media sources reported extensively on the heroism shown against the Axis powers in Greece, and propagated a view of modern Greek political allegiances. But it is also important to remember that the Greeks were not passive recipients of a Western-imposed image. During the nineteenth century, members of the nascent Greek nation had encouraged a representation of their country which remained so powerful that it continued to influence writing throughout much of the twentieth. It is to this that I turn my attention first.

(i) The Foundation of the Modern Greek Nation

A *nation* of people is not a natural phenomenon. Those who have sought to establish a nation-state face the twin tasks of legitimating it to the wider world community—by intellectually shaping the newly-independent territories to fit a pattern that is recognized internationally—and of ensuring that there is a group identity among the people within the country's geographical boundaries (Billig 1995; Hobsbawm 1992). In this section I examine how the people within the political creation called "Greece" came to be regarded as "Greek". At the time of independence in the nineteenth century, the identity of the people was open to question. I shall show how, within the Greek state following independence, the construction of being Greek was based on ideas circulating in the West about what qualified as a "nation". Those who controlled the intellectual direction of the new state encouraged the people of "the West" to view the Greeks positively, as part of Europe rather than of the "East". I shall argue that, one hundred years later, travel writers of the twentieth century were still following essential aspects of this view of Greekness when they formed their opinions and representations of the people they met.

At the end of the nineteenth century Ernest Renan was arguing that nations should be created without recourse to the idea of race. He was anxious to dismiss race as having "played no part in the constitution of modern nations" so that the legitimacy of the older European states would not be called into question: "the noblest countries, England, France, and Italy, are those where the blood is the most mixed" (Renan 1882:14). In the creation of a number of modern nations, race (in the sense of shared blood) was not deemed to matter so long as the people were—or could be made to seem—uniform in their cultural background and present traditions (Billig 1995:25-6, 70). Shared history and material heritage were used to provide a common experience for the nation-state, whether this collective past was real or imagined.

Both before and after it achieved political independence from the Ottoman Empire in the 1830s, Greece needed to justify its separation from the East and so sought to establish its credentials as a "European" country. As early as 1844, the Greek prime minister was—rather optimistically— declaring his country to be "in the centre of Europe" (Fleming 2000:1232). The past was chosen as the ground on which to wage the intellectual and rhetorical battle. At the time of the Greek War of Independence, many in the West viewed *ancient* Greece as the source of their own civilization. In the development of modern Europe, "science, progress, democracy, and commerce . . . could be traced as if they were a set of racial attributes to classical Greece" (Friedman 1992:839). Within Greece, it did not go unnoticed that

> Classicism as an ideology was popular among the upper and middle classes of the major European powers who were to support Greek national independence and guarantee it a secure life. (Hamilakis and Yalouri 1996:122)

The Greek middle class, already connected to the West through trade, appropriated the rhetoric of the West to meet their own aspirations to be admitted to the European "club". Selecting a history for a nation also involves forgetting. The recent *Turkish* past of Greece was ignored, and antiquity was emphasised. Mark Mazower has noted that, throughout the Balkans, newly-independent states have looked "to the medieval or classical past for their national roots, and encourage their historians to pass over the period of Ottoman rule as quickly as possible" (Mazower 2000:14). The culture of the Greek nation was to be that which was also claimed by the West as the antecedent of its own; the symbols of the new nation would be those monuments regarded by the West as the world's aesthetic pinnacle. The emphasis on the classical past was not merely designed to gain the general approval of the West, however, but was intended to signal the intentions of the new state to follow what were believed to be key values of the ancient world, such as democracy (Hamilakis and Yalouri 1996:127).

This promotion of the classical past by the Greek elite can be seen in architecture, political and administrative terminology, motifs on coins, titles of newspapers and magazines, and in the names given to ships, streets and communities (Peckham 2001:35; Yalouri 1993:12). Even the national language was changed.

> A high-flown neo-classical idiom seeking to bring the language of the descendants of Themistocles and Pericles back to their true heritage from the two millennia of slavery which had corrupted it. (Hobsbawm 1992:77)

Differing demands were made upon the physical remains of the history of Greece. Those of the classical period could be utilised to promote the idea that the population of Greece had a unity of past, and was European. Those of other periods needed to be swept away in order not to muddle the message, and in the name of progress. During the early years of the modern Greek state, the Byzantine period was considered by the ruling elite to have been one of corruption and foreign occupation, the government of which had been "authoritarian and theocratic" (Yalouri 1993:12). Hence, as I described in the previous chapter, the post-independence restoration of the Athenian Acropolis swept away monuments of the Byzantine and Turkish periods. Travel writers of the nineteenth and twentieth centuries were thus following the Greeks' lead when they found a "European" Acropolis, stripped of physical and metaphorical Turkish accretions.

In Greece, after a period of foreign rule, there was a particular need for what Anthony Smith has called the "rediscovery and revitalization of ethnic ties and sentiments" (1986:145). The task was to convince both those inside and outside Greece, not just that the Greeks had once been great, but that the modern residents were a single people, and the same people as in their former glory days. The people of Greece had already been renamed during the War of Independence, becoming "Hellenes" rather than being identified using a number of names signifying regional ties (Yalouri 2001:89-90). But the "new" Greek people had to be "rescued" from their Turkish elements. Greek intellectuals argued that "the modern state rested on an ancient foundation that had survived, relatively undamaged if also unappreciated, amongst the uneducated rural populations" (Herzfeld 1987:10). Elements of ancient Greek religion were identified as having been transformed into Christian traditions, beliefs, or saints. Anthony Smith has recently emphasised how organised religion had indeed played an important part in keeping Greek identity alive, through the "dense network of priests in the villages, [and] by the perennial daily ritual of the Church" (1986:115). The continuity argument was subscribed to, as I noted in the previous chapter, by Philhellenic observers of the nineteenth century. Whilst some were struck by "the absence of what was perceived as classical manners" (Todorova 1994:465), travellers could still view rural Greeks as the preservers of valued traditions. One example was Pitt-Rivers, who, according to John Davis, tended to "imply a continuity which is never justified." Pitt-Rivers wrote, for example, of "the fear of ungoverned female sexuality which has been an integral element of European folklore ever since prudent Odysseus lashed himself to the mast to escape the sirens" (Davis 1977:253). Even in the late twentieth century, however, some anthropologists and classicists were making quite uncritical assumptions about the continuity of traditions in Greece. For example, in their 1970 study of Greek rural beliefs I referred to in the previous chapter, Richard and Eva Blum argued that "there was much in the nineteenth century in Greece that would have been familiar to Pausanias and to Hesiod before him" (Blum and Blum 1970:6).

The historian Norman Davies has recently argued that, over the last two hundred years

> the impression has been created that everything "Western" is civilized, and that everything civilized is Western. By extension, or simply by default, anything vaguely Eastern or "Oriental" stands to be considered backward or inferior, and hence worthy of neglect. (Davies 1997:19)

As I have suggested, the new Greek nation had asserted its distinctiveness through promoting the cultural unity of its population, in opposition to what it was not: Turkish. There was a danger that Greece could be thought of as part of the Balkans, often regarded (then and since) as "an intermediate cultural zone between Europe and Asia—in Europe but not of it" (Mazower 2000:9). To some extent the perception of Greeks held by Westerners was caught up in this negative view. The depiction by twentieth century travel writers of, for example, the hardiness and violence exhibited by Cretans, has echoes of the "savage" representation of people elsewhere in the Balkans. However, in most instances this was read as a positive trait, part of the mentality of the *klefts* who had fought for freedom using guerilla tactics against the Turks and later, when known as *andartes*, in resisting the Germans. In his account of the foreign travellers murdered by "brigands" in 1870, Romilly Jenkins suggested that to many Greeks the *kleft* "seemed to unite in his person all that was most spirited and courageous in their national character" (Jenkins 1961:3). They were physically "of almost incredible hardihood, strength and resource" (Jenkins 1961:2). For historian Alan Clark, writing in 1962, the reaction of the Cretans to the Axis invasion of 1941 was based on "a whole tradition of mountain valour, of guerilla banditry, of rock and field craft and marksmanship that ran in the blood" (Clark 2000:79).

From the nineteenth century onwards the Greek ruling elite was remarkably successful in promoting a reading of Greece in which the immediate—Turkish—past was "lost" in favour of a history that would put the Greek people in the mainstream of European culture. The Greeks were encouraging the identification of the modern people with the period of their past most favoured within European education, as we shall see in the next section of this chapter. However, it is important to note that the use of the past has not been uncomplicated or unchanging. Although still looking to the ancient world for inspiration, the Metaxas regime of the 1930s emphasised Sparta over the more usual Athens "because of its perceived political organization, and ancient military events and virtues were favored over perceived intellectual or artistic achievements" (Brown and Hamilakis 2003:7). Some recent scholars have argued that the tendency of the West to superimpose the classical past on to modern Greece amounts to "metaphoric colonialism" (Fleming 2000:1221). But if there has been manipulation, it has been conducted on both sides, with Greece appropriating and exploiting the discourses and values of the West to establish an image that puts it among the civilized nations of Europe. The Greek political and cultural gaze continues to be directed West rather than East, as denoted by the country's membership of NATO and the EU. Recent publicity from the Greek National Tourist Organization promoted the country as the "birth place of Western civilization" (Travlou

2002:125). In 1990 Greeks reacted furiously when it was revealed that a foreign writer intended to omit Greece from his forthcoming book called *Europe: A History of its Peoples* (Davies 1997:43-4; Yalouri 2001:52-3).

Travel writers of the mid-twentieth century, as we shall see later, viewed the Greeks as impoverished but noble, preserving some of the traditions and practices of their illustrious ancestors. Ancient values— especially democracy—were transposed from the ancient to the modern people. All of these attributes are ultimately dependent upon that early nineteenth century positive discourse promoted at the time of Greek independence. Then, as later in the 1940s-60s, the Greeks could be seen as inheritors of the ancients only if they seemed disconnected from their recent (Turkish and non-European) past. Language, histories, and monuments, were adjusted accordingly. We can thus see the representation of the Greeks within various forms of twentieth century literature as part of a longstanding ideological process.

(ii) Classical Education and Knowledge

For many travel writers the primary meaning of "Greece" was *not* the state created in the 1830s as part of the slow unravelling of the Ottoman Empire, but the civilization that had existed in that country in ancient times. In 1809 Byron's travelling companion, John Cam Hobhouse, entered into his diary "first saw ancient Greece", after sailing between the islands of Cephalonia and Zakynthos (Minta 1998:4-5). To use the word "Greek" of a people did not so much denote half-Turkish peasants as recall the civilization which was believed to have formed the basis of European culture and society. Similarly, "Greek architecture" did not mean Turkish minarets or post-independence administrative buildings, but the temples, theatres and tombs of the classical past. In short, in both the nineteenth and twentieth centuries, when the words "Greece" or "Greek" were used, there was usually a word preceding them which was understood to be present: *ancient*. In his 1964 guidebook for the *Hellenic Traveller*, for example, Guy Pentreath gave his chapter about Delphi the subtitle "The Spiritual Centre of Greece". This is, clearly, a description which modern Orthodox Greeks would dispute, *unless*—as Pentreath obviously intended—"Greece" is understood to mean "ancient Greece" (1964:71).

In this section I shall be exploring how widespread knowledge was about the ancient Greeks among British people during the first seventy years of the twentieth century. To uncover the ideas that I believe were being transposed on to the modern people and country by travel writers to Greece, I shall also attempt to outline the representation during the same period of the ancient Greeks and their achievements. At times, however, it has been necessary for me to go as far back as the eighteenth century in order to trace the legacy of ideas about the ancient world inherited by travel writers of the 1940s. As Lorna Hardwick has said in relation to her study of classical influence:

> in looking at examples of modern reception it is necessary to consider the routes through which the ancient text or idea itself has passed and the way in which subsequent cultural assumptions filter modern representations. (2003:32)

In 1944 Demetrios Capetanakis suggested that "in this country modern Greeks are little known" (Hughes, H. 1944:135). However, he did not believe that the same was true for the ancient Greeks, for an Englishman "has done classics at school, perhaps also at the university, and Greece means for him a world of unreal perfection" (Hughes, H. 1944:135). A 1919 government pamphlet on classics argued that

> the history and thought of Greece and Rome are far nearer to us, far more real to us, than the history and thought of the centuries from the second to the sixteenth of our era. (Ministry of Reconstruction 1919:5)

Some of the travel writers whose works on Greece were published in Britain were no doubt educated in Australia, the USA, and elsewhere. Many, however, attended school in Britain. Here, therefore, I examine the extent to which knowledge of the classical past formed the education of British (and, more specifically, English) people from the late nineteenth century onwards.

In 1900 Classics occupied 40-60% of the curriculum time for those gentlemen who were educated in the fee-paying public schools (Stray 1992:28). A 1919 government report described "a classical education".

> Its main staple [is] the study of these languages [Greek and Latin], but it includes as important subsidiaries a considerable amount of "divinity" (Bible study), of history (ancient and modern), and of mathematics, and a modicum (possibly a small one) of natural science and of modern languages. (Ministry of Reconstruction 1919:9)

Schools for the new social-climbing industrial middle class of the nineteenth century aped this aristocratic model. Such education provided essential training for entrance into the universities of Oxford and Cambridge. In the last years of the nineteenth century, Compton Mackenzie's preparation for Oxford included the histories of Thucydides, Herodotus, and Xenophon; the oratory of Demosthenes; Greek tragedies; and Homer's *Odyssey* (Mackenzie 1960:8, 9, 12). In short, "a gentleman's education was, above all, a thorough training in the classics, which began at an early age and continued through to the university level" (Larson 1999:195).

An education based on classics was regarded as providing a number of benefits. R. W. Livingstone argued that the study of Greece and Rome was essential for understanding the modern world: "a man can hardly be said to be educated, who knows nothing of his spiritual ancestors" (Livingstone 1916:63-4). At around the same time, the Ministry of Reconstruction found more practical applications: "translation from and into Greek and Latin is an admirable training in precision of thought and clarity of expression" (1919:7). A classical education was often the key to career advancement. For example, in the 1850s an entry examination was introduced for the Indian Civil Service which put great weight on knowledge of classics, whereas "subjects which, on the face of it, might appear more useful to future administrators of India"—such as the subcontinent and its languages—counted for little (Larson 1999:197).

For girls, being educated during the later nineteenth century was somewhat different. Many of those who received formal schooling were taught at home by governesses or in small schools where the curriculum was unlikely to include ancient languages (Breay 1999:50). A number of fee-paying day and boarding schools for girls were established from the 1870s onwards, but, as Claire Breay comments, "girls who did go to school were taught far less Latin than boys and many were taught no Greek at all" (1999:49). A 1906 survey by the Classical Association confirmed that, in general, girls' schools devoted fewer hours on the timetable to Classics than did those for boys (Breay 1999:52-3). Of course, for members of some social classes in Britain, a classical education was never a reality, or even perhaps an aspiration. Free education for all at elementary and secondary levels was introduced by the state in the late nineteenth and early twentieth centuries respectively, but these schools for the "working class" concentrated on teaching the rudiments of the three Rs ("Reading, Writing, 'Rithmetic").

In the first decades of the twentieth century, the British school system for boys in particular came under fire for its failure to sufficiently embrace newer subjects such as natural sciences and modern languages. This was due in part to the perceived failure of British industry to meet the demands of the First World War (Stray 1992:49). The authors of the government's official post-war report were forced to agree that "in many schools of the older type more time is needed for instruction in natural science." In such situations, "the time allotted to Classics must be reduced" (Ministry of Reconstruction 1919:12, 14). It was recommended that less time be devoted to grammar and composition, and to "assist progress by the aid of translations" (Ministry of Reconstruction 1919:14).

> Those who go no further will at least have been introduced to interesting portions of such authors as Homer, Herodotus, Caesar and Cicero, and will have some comprehension of ancient languages and ancient history. (Ministry of Reconstruction 1919:14)

If such proposals were adopted, the effects would inevitably spread to the universities, particularly Oxford and Cambridge, whose own curricula were so dependent upon prior knowledge of the ancient world, and more precisely upon competence in ancient languages. Indeed, the compulsory Greek requirement for Oxbridge entrance was ended within a few years of the First World War (Stray 1998:165-6, 267-8). Predictably, the result was that the number of schools teaching their pupils Greek dwindled (Jenkyns 1980:64). The founders of the Classical Association, formed as a defensive body in 1903, saw that the writing was on the wall, and argued that "classicists should reorganize curricula before it was taken out of their hands" (Stray 1998:253-4).

However, the perceived value of classics was also changing. In 1911, it could still be maintained by J. C. Stobart that Greece provided "fixed canons in matters of taste" (Stray 1998:289). In later decades absolute values were less often being claimed for classical culture. By the 1950s the primary value of Latin was often said to be the "mental discipline" it engendered (Stray 1998:279, 295). As a result, the 1950s "O" Level examination consisted largely of translating (in both directions) and questions on grammar, but included little on the cultural background to the ancient texts (Forrest 1996:11). But in 1959, at a meeting of the Association for the Reform of Latin Teaching, William Thompson made a plea "not for an academic study of classical Latin and Greek but a distillation of the Graeco-Roman part of our heritage through the teacher" (Forrest 1996:1). Such "progressives" were arguing that the classics currently being taught was too narrowly focused on the few who needed it for university entrance, and that it would be desirable to include more translation into English and less composition in Latin (Forrest 1996:11). 1960, however, saw the ending of the requirement of a qualification in Latin in order to study at Oxford or Cambridge. Not long afterwards, Her Majesty's Inspectors reported their concern at the steady decline in the number of candidates offered by schools for public examinations in both Greek and Latin (Forrest 1996:13, 15).

The first fifty years of the twentieth century had witnessed the gradual movement of classics from the centre to the margins of education. Nevertheless, the survey I have presented here explains why the majority of those who produced travel writing from the 1940s until the early 1970s were likely to have travelled to Greece with greater knowledge of the ancient Greeks than of the modern people. This helps us to understand why many found it difficult to associate with the modern Greeks without forming comparisons—explicit or otherwise—with their ancient forebears. But who were these ancient Greeks that travel writers found lurking in the shadows behind the modern people of Greece?

Above all, the ancient Greeks were regarded as the producers of the pinnacle of world art. From the Renaissance onwards, in Western Europe ancient sculpture had been the standard by which achievement in the visual arts was judged. But the appreciation and emulation of classical antiquity assumed a new intensity in the Britain of the nineteenth century. Major artists including Lord Leighton, who became President of the Royal Academy, devoted the majority of their output to recognisably Greek subjects, whether titled as such or not (Jones et al. 1996). Public institutions formed collections of casts of classical sculpture in order to train and refine the taste of artists, craftsmen and manufacturers. Indeed, it is believed that "by the mid-nineteenth century there was hardly a sizable town in Europe or North America that did not somewhere possess the cast of at least one of Elgin's marbles" (Beard 2002:18).

A major turning point in the Western European obsession with the ancient world had occurred in the late eighteenth century: a focus on the ancient Greeks rather than the Romans. In a book published in 1764, Johann Winckelmann had attempted to distil the features of specifically Greek, rather than classical, art. Winckelmann concluded that the Greek sculptors of the fifth century BC had arrived at an ability to capture ideal beauty, rather than representing the world as it is (Turner, F. 1981:42).

Winckelmann's characterization of fifth and fourth century sculpture—"a noble simplicity and a calm grandeur"—was hugely influential right through to the twentieth century (Jenkyns 1991:87). It was the work of Winckelmann which paved the way for Greece to become not merely admired, but an ideal against which aesthetics—both ancient and modern—were to be judged. In the nineteenth century Greek sculpture came to be viewed as the antithesis of the "harshness, materialism, and sham" of modern life (Turner, F. 1981:36).

Classical *architecture* was likewise universally known and used as "the common architectural language, inherited from Rome, of nearly the whole civilized world in the five centuries between the Renaissance and our own time" (Summerson 1964:7). At the turn of the eighteenth and nineteenth centuries, architects were looking to a more "authentic" *Greek* style, just as Winckelmann had in ancient sculpture (Jenkyns 1991:48, 52; Watkin and Windsor Liscombe 2000:4-6). In this they were aided and inspired by *The Antiquities of Athens*, the result of the two-year visit by James Stuart and Nicholas Revett from March 1751. The volume covering the major monuments of the city of Athens was published in 1789, providing representations designed to be "accurate" rather than "picturesque" (Brothers 1997:114, 116). During the nineteenth century caryatids closely modelled on those of the Erechtheion appeared on the exterior of a church (H. W. and W. Inwood's St. Pancras, London) and in the interior of a bank (Sir John Soane's Bank of England Dividend Office); the Acropolis-style Ionic capital was eschewed by C. R. Cockerell for the entrance to the Ashmolean Museum in favour of one he had recorded himself at Bassae (Crook 1972: 133, 138; Jenkyns 1991: 59-60, 63-4, 67-70). Across the British Empire, public buildings and monuments in a more generalised Greco-Roman style, designed to symbolise dignity and dominance, continued to be built during the second half of the nineteenth century and into the twentieth (Jenkyns 1980:333; Larson 1999:223; Stray 1998:63).

As in art and architecture, from the late eighteenth century interest in classical literature shifted away from Roman writers like Cicero and Horace (Crook 1972:42; Turner, F. 1989:62). The great Athenian playwrights—Aeschylus, Sophocles, Euripides—became "figures worthy of attention and emulation in the present" (Turner, F. 1981:29). The second half of the nineteenth century saw a number of productions of Greek plays around Britain, and special trains were run from London in 1882 for Sophocles' *Ajax*, the first of the ongoing series of tragedies and comedies performed in Greek at Cambridge (Stray 1999:30, 36; Taplin 1989:56). Richard Jenkyns points out that

> Victorian novelists could sprinkle allusions to Greek tragedy through their books without obvious artificiality because they lived in an age when there were people who found in these plays a powerful consolation for their distresses. (Jenkyns 1980:96)

The high regard in which Greek literature was held continued into the twentieth century. The authors of the 1919 report on *The Classics in British Education* stated that "the literature of Greece is the finest in the world, though our own may come next to it" (Ministry of Reconstruction 1919:6). According to Oliver Taplin, writing in 1989, Greek myths and stories became "a more significant ingredient in the creative cauldron since 1900 than at any other time since the first century BC." This resurgent interest was partly due to "important developments in anthropology and psychology, developments which gave new, hidden meanings to the myths" (Taplin 1989:93, 95). Major writers including W. B. Yeats, Ezra Pound, Eugene O'Neill, and T. S. Eliot, found inspiration in Greek tragedy (Jenkyns 1980:94, 111; Taplin 1989:57-8). Greek myths and drama were also interpreted in a new medium by film directors including Jean Cocteau, Jules Dassin, Michael Cacoyannis and Pier Paolo Pasolini, with a number of low-budget "Hercules" tales also appearing in the 1960s (Nisbet 2006:49ff; Winkler 2001:72ff, 332).

In its political system Athens has not always been regarded as a state to be admired, since, as Mary Beard and John Henderson remark, "democracy itself has become a generally embraced and positive concept only in very recent times" (1995:89). At the beginning of the nineteenth century, the recent American and French Revolutions had led to renewed British interest in ancient "democratic" politics. But it was ancient Sparta that was regarded as a "strong, stable polity immune from the political unrest, party factions, and turbulent leadership that had marked Athenian political life" (Turner, F. 1981:189-90). However, George Grote's *History of Greece*, published in twelve volumes between 1846 and 1856, transformed the Victorian representation of ancient Athens (Jenkyns 1980:14; Turner, F. 1981:213). At a time when the British Empire was burgeoning, the views of such aristocratic ancient authors as Plato, Aristotle and Thucydides on maintaining a system of democracy in the face of the potentially anarchic mass of the people provided "useful guidelines as to the proper way for an elite to rule 'inferior' people for their own good" (Larson 1999:208, 209). Many Victorians came to identify themselves with the ancient Greeks.

> The perception of a close relationship between the political history of ancient Athens and Great Britain had emerged as an almost unquestioned assumption for numerous British intellectuals. (Turner, F. 1981:189, 10-1)

This continued into the First World War, when Pericles' "Funeral Speech" was used in recruitment drives to emphasise the importance of fighting for freedom (Taplin 1989:204). It was not only Greece of the high classical period that provided inspiration in warfare. The idea that Homer's account of the Trojan War promoted heroic behaviour stretched back well into the nineteenth century. Even in 1915 Compton Mackenzie encountered a general on campaign at Gallipoli—near the site of ancient Troy— searching for an allusion in his pocket-sized copy of the *Iliad* in Greek (1960:22).

By 1900, in contrast to its earlier positive press, Athens' ancient rival Sparta had lost the nineteenth century propaganda battle. In 1916 R. W. Livingstone was typical in describing Sparta as

> that country of austere and Puritan heroes, who thought a state could exist without a civilisation, and, banishing equally art and commerce, literature and gold and silver, have left the world doubtful whether to admire the virtues, or to despise the narrow efficiency of, these human ants. (1916:188)

By the 1930s the contemporary people most likely to be identified with Spartans—by themselves and others—were the Nazis. Hitler, for example, stated his admiration for the Spartan system of communal military training, subjection of the inferior helots, and exposure of weakling babies (Rawson 1969:342; Taplin 1989:214-5). Elizabeth Rawson opened her pioneering examination of *The Spartan Tradition in European Thought* by outlining the view that prevailed in the late 1960s.

> Ancient Sparta: a militaristic and totalitarian state, holding down an enslaved population, the helots, by terror and violence, educating its young by a system incorporating all the worst features of the traditional English public school, and deliberately turning its back on the intellectual and artistic life of the rest of Greece. Such, at least, is the picture, if any, which mention of the name consciously or unconsciously conjures up in the minds of most people in this country today. The liberal democratic tradition that dominates modern English thought has very naturally tended

to idealize Sparta's great rival, democratic Athens; and its consequent distrust of Sparta was reinforced by a reaction against a very different set of ideas, particularly prominent in Germany where admiration for Sparta reached a fantastic conclusion under the Nazis. (Rawson 1969:1)

The identification of Germany-Sparta-dictatorship and Britain-Athens-democracy was fully exploited during both world wars to make sense of the conflicts and to provide exemplars for behaviour.

At present we, who are at war with an adventurer nation, can read Demosthenes with greater understanding, as he denounces the designs of an adventurer king: and as he warns the Athenians of their unpreparedness, and implores them to awake to the situation, can recognise that his words might be applied to other times beside the fourth century, and other democracies besides Athens. (Livingstone 1916:189)

In 1941 Gilbert Murray "compared the Second World War with the Peloponnesian War, England of course playing the role of liberal and democratic Athens" (Rawson 1969:365-6).

Grote in political thought and history, Winckelmann in art, Stuart and Revett in architecture, had placed fifth century *Athens* at the apex of Greek achievement. The apex of Athenian achievement—architectural forms and sculpture, tragic theatre, the democratic system—had become an inspiration for modern political and cultural projects. For much of the twentieth century the idea of Britain being in "debt" to ancient Greece was as current as it had been for Philhellenes during the War of Independence. In the midst of the Second World War Hilda Hughes was writing of the "ideal of Democracy" as one of Greece's "gifts" to the modern world (1944:11). Francis Noel-Baker maintained in his children's book *Looking at Greece* that "Europe's politics, philosophy, architecture, mathematics, science, and even her music originated in Greece" (1967:61). It is, then, hardly surprising to find that travel to Greece during the mid-twentieth century was often inspired by the perceived importance of its ancient history. Compton Mackenzie, for example, regarded it as "vital to the future of our country that her youth should visit the country where our Western civilisation was born" (Mackenzie 1960:171).

The concepts of what constituted the civilization of ancient Greece were in part propagated—to travel writers and others—via histories and textbooks. As Christopher Stray has argued, "textbooks are the media of the classical message, the forms which organize its content" (1998:54).

Two books on history and culture, which ran into many editions in the period after 1945, will serve here to illustrate how the ancient Greek achievement was viewed in Britain. *The Greek Commonwealth*, first published in 1911 but still being reprinted in the 1960s, was intended by author Alfred Zimmern to be "useful to students" as well as the "general reader" (1911:9). Zimmern was explicit about the slippage of terms that occurred when thinking about the ancient world.

> To us in the North, if we are book-learned and home-keeping, Greece and Italy spell Athens and Rome. They are associated in our minds with a host of inherited ideas, with Art and Freedom and Law and Empire. They are familiar to us as the cradle of some of the strongest forces in our national life, as the first and most congenial home of our distinctively Western civilization. (Zimmern 1911:17)

Zimmern adopted this focus on the ancient city, and on *Athens* in particular.

> The City-State was the centre and inspiration of all their most characteristic achievements, culminating in the great outpouring of literature and art and practical energy, of great men and great deeds, in fifth-century Athens. (1911:58).

Yet for all this, Zimmern laid claim to the ancient Greeks as a pastoral people.

> [The Greek City] is in essence not a marketing or manufacturing centre, but an overgrown agricultural village . . . The full-grown city never forgot its country origin, nor did its citizens lose contact with its fields outside the walls. (1911:84)

In attempting to establish the elements which led to Greek democracy, Zimmern began with the premise that "the Greeks, like most peoples in similar climates, were sociable and gregarious and enjoyed mixing in large companies" (1911:61). He believed that the early settlers in Greece were egalitarian by instinct.

> [They] followed their leader in time of war and accepted the decisions of his council of wise men; but they did not regard one family or brotherhood or section of the community as any better than another. (1911:88)

When Zimmern discussed the achievements of the dictatorial rulers of the seventh and sixth centuries BC, he made clear his view that the natural

state of the ancient people of Greece—and the apogee of the Greek state—
was the democracy of Athens.

> In the development which we are tracing—the growth of the influences
> which culminated in the political life of fifth-century Athens—the tyrants
> are an interlude. (1911:125-6)

The Spartan system, on the other hand, was dismissed as imposing "a
discipline so strict and inhuman that no race of human beings can be loyal
to it in their hearts" (1911:132).

The history of J. C. Stobart's book *The Glory that was Greece* parallels
Zimmern's in being issued in 1911 and reprinted right into the 1960s. But
Stobart's subject was less the ancient Greek political system than its
cultural achievements. The original preface has Stobart squaring up to a
world in which "the Greek language has now, probably for ever, lost its
place in the the curriculum of secondary education for the greater part of
our people." Nevertheless, he felt that "there has always been a genuinely
cultivated public to whom Greek was unknown, and it is undoubtedly very
much larger in this generation" (Stobart 1911:viii). Stobart's thesis was
that the fifth century BC represented the pinnacle of Greek civilization.
The rendering of the human figure during the earlier Geometric phase was
described as "careless and clumsy", whereas in the "glorious fifth century"
Greek art arrived "near to perfection" (1911:56, 70, 103). Likewise, in
architecture Stobart believed the Parthenon to have been the "goal" at
which earlier attempts to construct temples had been aiming (1911:107-8).
Stobart conceded that "so entirely does Athens focus upon herself the
culture of the fifth century, we are apt to forget that Athens was not
Greece" (1911:168). Stobart therefore went out of his way to find praise
for Sparta's political system—"which gave her the best, or at any rate the
most stable, government in Greek history"—but he found in the Spartan
lifestyle the seeds of the city's downfall.

> It made the Spartans oppressive and unjust when they had to govern an
> empire. The typical Spartan is narrow-minded, superstitious, and covetous,
> but he is always brave, patriotic, and often chivalrous. Sparta has left us no
> art or literature, but she has left us an extraordinary experiment (for a
> warning) of aristocratic communism combined with unfettered militarism.
> (1911:83, 94)

Sparta and Athens were viewed as cities of contrast.

> Sparta drilled, orderly, efficient, and dull; Athens free, noisy, fickle, and brilliant. Sparta's watchword in history is Eunomia (order); the motto of Athens is Eleutheria (liberty) and Parrhesia (free speech and free thought). (1911:94)

Though their books focused upon different aspects of its history, Zimmern and Stobart shared a vision of ancient Greece. The Greeks were cultured and democratic by nature. The ancient city was paramount, yet the people had their roots in the land. The city-state of Athens was more important than Sparta, and the achievements of the fifth century overshadowed those of preceding and subsequent periods. In order to understand the aesthetic achievement of fifth century Athens—celebrated by Zimmern, Stobart and those who travelled to Greece in the twentieth century to worship at the Parthenon—I examine here two more detailed accounts of the Acropolis.

Gerhart Rodenwaldt's *The Acropolis* was first translated into English in 1930, with its second edition appearing in 1957. Rodenwaldt placed the Athenian monuments at the zenith of Greek—and world—aesthetics. The rock of the Acropolis was "firm foundation for the most beautiful edifices ever raised by the hand of man" (Rodenwaldt 1930:10). He conceded that the loss of its original painted colour robbed the modern viewer of seeing the Parthenon in its ancient glory, but praised its current appearance.

> The action of weather and atmosphere, together with the bright light and the fine grain of the stone, has given the marble a golden brown tinge which has been compared to the colour of ripening corn. (1930:34)

The Temple of Athena Nike had become a "rare jewel", whilst the Erechtheion presented a "picturesque unity" to the modern eye (1930:47, 52-3). In 1963 the Classical Association published a supplement to its journal *Greece and Rome*, entitled *Parthenos and Parthenon*. The contributors to this volume, edited by G. T. W. Hooker, likewise described the Parthenon as a work of art. Alison Burford, for example, maintained that the whole construction was controlled by the sculptor Pheidias as a frame for his own work (Hooker 1963:25). A symbolic viewing of the Acropolis was suggested by Russell Meiggs as he attempted to set the building project within the context of the period of peace and power for Athens following the Persian Wars. The Parthenon was the "creation of a free democracy, initiated, controlled, and approved by the popular assembly and its judicial organs" (1963:45). The contributors to *Parthenos and Parthenon*, Rodenwaldt, and indeed writers of more general ancient history books such as Stobart, all viewed the Parthenon as an artistic creation more than a building, and as the apogee of ancient Greek architectural achievement. Further, the Acropolis represented the pinnacle of the whole of ancient Greek culture: built by the most significant city (Athens), and during the most significant time (the fifth century).

As I suggested in the previous chapter, the extant remains of Sparta received a very different press to those of Athens in early twentieth century travel accounts. It was, again, Winckelmann who had, in his book of 1764, first postulated a link between the presence or absence of democracy and quality of art (Ferris 2000:30). For later historians, Sparta's ugly military system was mirrored in what remained at the site in the 1900s. Paul MacKendrick, writing in the early 1960s, noted that archaeologists "never expected its ruins to be spectacular" (1962:147). In the excavations conducted there by the British from 1906, for example:

> evidence was found, in the artistic decline of votive offerings, of the metamorphosis of Sparta into a military state, with stifled aesthetic interests, in the sixth century. (MacKendrick 1962:149)

As we shall see in the next chapter, travel writers of the mid-twentieth century would often inscribe Sparta, like Athens, in line with its status within contemporary classical learning.

With the monuments of Athens as aesthetic wonder and demonstration of how creativity flourishes under a democracy, and Sparta's relics a warning of the stunted output that comes with dictatorship, other sites in Greece were regarded as having their own individual values and attributes. The "Handbook" for the 1963 series of *Swans Hellenic Cruises*, edited by Sir Mortimer Wheeler, is suggestive of how the financially better-off tourists who travelled with this company in the post-Second World War period were directed to view these sites. For example, the first four paragraphs of the chapter on Olympia concern the games, whilst the section on Delphi begins by emphasising the natural surroundings, continuing with its ancient religious significance and the oracle (Wheeler 1963:39, 43). One year before in publication date, Helen Hill Miller's guide to Greece contained chapter headings which promoted similar aspects of these sites: "Delphi: Political Prophecy", and "Olympia: The Greek Games" (Hill Miller 1962). To return to those engaged in a Swan Hellenic Cruise, a visit to the Temple of Poseidon at Sounion was recommended for three reasons.

The coastal scenery on the way is excellent, as is the road itself; at Sounion it is not too difficult in imagination to sense the effect upon the mind of the beauty of the white marble temple high and serene above the sea in the days of its reassuring service to the seamen of Athens; and the view, out over the island-studded waters, east, south, and west, is characteristically Greek. (Wheeler 1963:36)

As in so many other guide books, the temple at Sounion is here not regarded as important because of its history, and its own aesthetic merit is not considered to be of the first rank—it "may not itself have been a rare masterpiece" (Wheeler 1963:36)—but it is the combination of location and ruin that receives praise.

At Mycenae and Knossos respectively, Schliemann and Evans had claimed to have uncovered not merely important traces of ancient civilization but sites associated with mythical protagonists. But instead of continuing the search for connections between myth and archaeological remains, Schliemann's successor as excavator of Mycenae, Christos Tsountas, was "content to see potential origins for the Homeric stories in Mycenaean times, while recognising that other factors have resulted in the formation of the poems" (Fitton 1995:105-6). The accuracy of Homer received a further academic blow in the 1950s, when Hilda Lorimer concluded that the *Iliad* and *Odyssey* could not be said to represent any one historical society (Fitton 1995:204). By the 1960s Schliemann's Agamemnon had been replaced with an altogether more general assertion that Swan travellers could see what must have been "royal tombs" (Wheeler 1963:51). Following Schleimann's lead, Arthur Evans was convinced that myths could be read in the ruins of Knossos. For example, the scenes on the frescoes that he uncovered suggested to him that the stories of young Athenians sent as sacrifices to the Minotaur might have their origins in real sports involving bulls (Fitton 1995:131). During his lifetime Evans had enforced his interpretations on the academic community; his death in 1941 meant that the 1963 Swan Handbook was reporting, in a "Postscript" to its chapter on Knossos, dissenting voices as a recent development (Wheeler 1963:68). Nevertheless, travellers were informed that the Minotaur story was "a vestigial reminder of great bull-fights", and that the "maze of passages in the palace of Knossos . . . perhaps generated the very concept of a labyrinth" (1963:67).

In examining guidebooks, histories and education curricula, we need to recognize the difficulties in assessing the extent of knowledge about the ancient world amongst British people of the twentieth century. Christopher

Stray, who has studied the classics in education in greater depth than anyone else in recent years, queries how much absorption and understanding even public schoolboys possessed at the end of their schooling. In Stray's view the majority would have left school "with only a few half-remembered tags and lines learned off by heart" (1998:59). The pressures I described earlier in the chapter for greater teaching of "new" subjects such as science, led almost inevitably to a decline in the depth with which aspects of the ancient past were studied. As early as 1923, a book of passages from ancient authors in translation was intended for

> the ordinary educated reader, as well as for pupils at the universities and in the upper forms of schools, who will never learn the language but need not be left in total ignorance of the literature and thought of Greece. (Livingstone 1923:v)

Interest in the ancient world was not, however, restricted to those who could be expected to have had an extensive formal education. In 1917 the founder of the Workers' Educational Association claimed that "working people are displaying an increasing interest in such subjects as Greek Democracy and Greek Moral and Political Thought" (Ministry of Reconstruction 1919:16). In the latter half of the nineteenth century, the banners and membership certificates of various trade unions had adopted classical imagery. In this way, working class people were appropriating symbols from the "High Art" of the Victorian elite, but this does not necessarily imply that all of the union members were familiar with the culture from which these ultimately derived. Many referents can be "read" at differing levels, dependent upon the consumer's knowledge. For example, when viewing the external architecture of the British Museum, those steeped in the classical tradition might notice the choice of column that had been made in the design; but to the majority, it would merely "announce that this was a monument of cultural authority" (Stray 1998:64). Richard Jenkyns has characterized the classical influence in nineteenth century architecture as comprising two strands: that based on the "scholarly" interest in the monuments of Greece (i.e. the Greek Revival), and that which was a continuation of the "broad classical tradition of Europe" (Jenkyns 1991:19). The extensive use of such architectural features as columns and pediments in, for example, Victorian mausoleums and shopfronts, was an expression of monumentality using an ongoing vaguely-classical vocabulary. Such uses did not denote a detailed knowledge of ancient history in their spectators or creators.

However, as I suggested in chapter one, the writers and publishers of mid-twentieth century travel writing often assumed a quite considerable knowledge of ancient Greece in their readers. Many writers apparently retained powerful memories of their British classical education. In *Greece in My Life* Compton Mackenzie recalled how, by the age of thirteen, he "could, if I wished, put twenty lines of Shakespeare into Greek iambics in less than an hour" (Mackenzie 1960:8). For many, ancient Greece was with them from youth to old age. In chapter three I shall demonstrate that travel writers' descriptions of particular sites and monuments are connected to the interpretations we have seen offered by contemporary histories and guidebooks. For example, the focus within travel writing on the remains of Athens, and the corresponding denigration of what was left of Sparta, is a reflection of what was perceived as the relative importance and merits of those ancient cities. In the descriptions of Athens, the emphasis placed upon the aesthetic virtues of the Parthenon—rather than other possible significances—is related to its portrayal as a masterpiece by historians of ancient Greece. I shall be arguing in chapter four that the representation of the modern people of Greece within mid-twentieth century travel accounts is likewise congruent with the views of ancient history that were disseminated through the education system and textbooks of the time. Most obviously, we have seen that there were many literary precedents for travel writers to describe the people they met as figures from myth and history, and to suggest that beliefs and practices were ancient survivals. More generally, however, the willingness of travel writers to form a positive image of the modern Greeks came from a perceived shared culture, and the debt owed by the West to their ancient forebears. As we have seen in this chapter, during the majority of the twentieth century ancient Greece was regularly asserted to be the origin of Western culture. European—British—art, architecture, poetry, drama, and political ideology, were believed to have been based on classical exemplars. There was also transference from ancient to modern of certain perceived character traits. The identification of the modern Greeks as naturally democratic stemmed from the emphasis that the history books placed upon the ancient Athenian political system. As I shall now show in the last section of this chapter, Allied writings and propaganda from 1940 onwards also promoted particular readings of the past in order to emphasise the heroism of the Greeks and their democratic credentials as natural allies of the West.

(iii) Anglo-Greek Relations: The Second World War Onwards

In April 1941 the Swastika was flying on the Acropolis. But the courage and resilience shown by the Greeks in resisting Axis aggression up to that point received due recognition in the West. Greece had entered the Second World War on 28th October 1940, when the Greek leader Metaxas rejected Mussolini's demand that Italian troops be stationed on his nation's soil. The Greek army then succeeded in driving the invading Italians back into Albania. Greeks had continued to resist when faced with the might of Hitler's much greater military resources. In planning their airborne invasion of Crete, for example, German commanders had believed that the locals would readily surrender (MacDonald 1995:77). Instead, the Cretans reacted with "a wild, unreasoning anger which, shaped by a tradition of guerilla warfare against the Ottoman Empire, gave no quarter" (MacDonald 1995:153). Civilians attacked the landing paratroopers with anything that came to hand: knives, sticks, antique guns, then weapons looted from the enemy or given to them by evacuating Allied soldiers (MacDonald 1995:176-8, 194, 279).

The Greek campaign was widely reported in newspapers of many countries so that in 1943 Derek Patmore felt able to comment that "today everyone knows the heroic story of Greek resistance" (1943:9). The initial Greek action against the Italians was said to have "discouraged and then distracted the enemy" from its campaign in North Africa (Garnett 1942:7). Though later generations of historians have expressed doubts, at the time it was generally believed that Greek resistance had caused a crucial delay in Germany's planned invasion of Russia (Garnett 1942:62; Hadjipateras and Fafalios 1995:282-5; Horlington 1991:72; Hughes, H. 1944:13). As explained by Ernest Bevin in 1946, the British government felt that British morale had been bolstered.

> At a time when everything and all hope seemed lost, Greece made available not only her territory but also her arms and military effort at the disposal of the Allied struggle. (Hadjipateras and Fafalios 1995:285)

With the battle lost, reports of Greek resistance to the Nazi occupation of their country began to emerge. Individuals and whole communities were willing to commit their lives and the few resources they had to the assistance of British soldiers and agents. The Cretan George Psychoundakis described such work in his memoirs as his "sacred duty" (Psychoundakis 1955:46). British commando Stanley Moss, in his classic account of the kidnapping of the German commander on Crete, *Ill Met by Moonlight*, was suitably appreciative of the reception he received from local people: "it was really heart-warming to see all these kind and enthusiastic faces and to feel that we were among such genuine friends" (2001:46).[6] Officially at least, there was belief in the loyalty of all Greeks to the Allied cause. The account of the campaign in Greece published by the British government stated of the Cretans that "there was not a Quisling among them" during the invasion of the island (Garnett 1942:44). However, the price for such allegiance could be terrible. Discovery of aid given to British agents often resulted in the destruction of whole villages (Beevor 1992:262; Psychoundakis 1955:223, 230, 231, 284-6). During the occupation the economy collapsed, unemployment was extensive, and in the famine of the winter 1941/2 Athens witnessed "the worst scenes of starvation seen in occupied Europe outside the concentration camps" (Mazower 2001:22). In his account of his experiences as a boy living in occupied Greece, Elias Yialouris recalled watching his mother's death from starvation and, as a reward for joining the resistance, having "a full stomach for the first time in two years" (Rowland 2000:48-9, 80).

The Allies needed some help identifying—and identifying with—these unexpectedly steadfast Greeks. The *War Illustrated* reported the message sent by Lt. Gen. Sir Thomas Blamey to his forces in Greece.

> In Australia we know little of this valiant nation. I am sure that as you get to know the Greeks the magnificent courage of their resistance will impress you more and more. It is not unlikely that the action of this small and noble nation may prove in the end to be the beginning of the final downfall of Nazi tyranny. (Hadjipateras and Fafalios 1995:175-6)

Accounts published in Britain during the war years, including by the government itself, emphasised the qualities the Greeks had shown during the fighting, the validity of the failed attempt by the British to save Greece from the Germans, and tried to demystify the modern Greek race. Hilda Hughes' edited volume was intended to counter an attitude perceived as prevalent amongst scholars of Greece.

> Instead of seeing the Greek who stands before them as he [*sic*] really is, they fold him in so many verses they know by heart, in so many names of heroes, poets, philosophers or artists they admire, in so many memories from their school or college life. (Hughes, H. 1944:136)

Although various contributors to Hughes' book acknowledged the somewhat backward nature of the country and its people, to help the reader identify with modern Greece this was either explained away, extolled as a virtue, or described as in the process of changing. For example, although it was conceded that since the beginning of the twentieth century there had been "only two perceptible periods of complete democratic harmony", the reader was assured that "whatever domestic difficulties of political opinion may exist in Greece they are certainly no sharper there than in almost every country in Europe today" (Hughes, H. 1944:32, 185). The simple way of life of the Greeks was made to seem a virtue, resulting in hardiness (Hughes, H. 1944:18). Great strides were said to have been made in education, industry and social welfare, and more were not to be expected given the short period of time since independence (Hughes, H. 1944:33-4). The apparent strangeness of the Orthodox Church was dismissed as being superficial: the appearance of the priests "obscures their brotherhood with the Western priesthood and the common purpose which inspires the Church in East and West alike" (Hughes, H. 1944:43). As well as minimising the differences between Greece and the West, the book gave an impression of the Greeks as true friends of the British—in peace and war. Just as pre-conflict travellers found peasant hospitality, Britons on the run from the Germans received help (Hughes, H. 1944:11, 19, 47).

In another book published in the 1940s, Stanley Casson's purpose was likewise to collapse the differences between *Greece and Britain*. He claimed that, via Byzantium, the two peoples had the same cultural base (Casson 1943:38). In the nineteenth century the British assisted the Greeks to gain independence, and subsequently reintroduced them to the idea of democracy: "from the British they acquired a knowledge of the workings of the British Constitution, on which, in due course, they based their own" (Casson 1943:108). Ideas derived from the ancient Greeks were passed on via the British to other peoples of the world: "it is on the Greek model that the British Admiralty founded our immense system of world-wide charts, accessible to all men [*sic*] for the safety of all sailors" (Casson 1943:15). Thus, in their preservation and transmission of culture and democratic ideals, the British were viewed by Casson as equal in importance to the modern Greeks as inheritors of the classical past. It was therefore natural that the two modern countries should be side-by-side against the Axis powers: "in the war of 1914-1918 Greece and Britain were allies . . . and once again in this war the two peoples are fighting together" (Casson 1943: jacket).

Casson's argument of a long history of contact between Greeks and Britons was pertinent only if the population of Greece was assumed to have remained ethnically or culturally the same through the centuries. Some of the writers in Hughes' book acknowledged the variety of influences apparent in modern Greeks: "Minoan" costume on Crete, trousers from "Islam", Italian words, English cricket in Corfu (Hughes, H. 1944:1-7). This celebration of the strength and virtue of a mixed cultural background seems a particularly Churchillian response to the Nazi promotion of Aryanism. But it could nevertheless be maintained that "their ancestors built the Parthenon" (Hughes, H. 1944:141). This connection between ancient and modern was achieved by collapsing history. For a Greek, stated Helle Georgiadis,

> the history of Greece in the last 1,000 years seems telescoped to him into a shorter time, because of the occupation of Greece for several centuries by a people alien to her thought. (Hughes, H. 1944:42)

The entire Turkish period was wiped away. The Greek people had had minimal contact with and were not influenced by the Ottoman occupiers, and the traditions of the preceding Byzantine period—which had preserved much from ancient Greece—were kept "pure" to the present day. Stanley Casson's view of the Turkish occupation was similar.

> The ancient conceptions of freedom and justice were not dead. They may have been dormant since [the fall of Constantinople to the Turks in] 1453 but they had not perished . . . the Greek nature had not changed. (Casson 1943:95)

The actions of the Greeks in the Second World War could be seen as part of a pattern. Modern Greek history offered a series of occasions in which the people fought for their independence. In 1843, for example, the Greeks demanded a constitution of their monarch because they "wanted to govern themselves" (Hughes, H. 1944:31). In the conflict of the 1940s the Greeks showed that they "loved freedom and counted not their bodies dear" (Hughes, H. 1944:12). The "few fought against the many", these "descendants of Themistocles and Miltiades" (Hughes, H. 1944:33). Hughes' volume was by no means unusual in its use of comparison to classical heroes. In her book published during the war Dilys Powell described how the Greeks had seized the opportunity to "prove themselves of the same fabric as the men who fought the Persian hosts" (Powell 1941:179). As Ian Macgregor Morris has shown, the invocation of battles from the ancient Persian Wars as inspiration for contemporary Greek conflicts dates from at least the end of the eighteenth century. At that time, the heroes of Thermopylae were used as exemplars of the qualities of bravery, desire for liberty from a foreign foe, and preparedness for martyrdom that were considered necessary to attain Greek independence (Macgregor Morris 2000:220-2). Leaders in the Second World War readily adopted such comparisons. Charles de Gaulle saluted:

> the Greek people who are fighting for freedom. 25th March 1941 finds Greece at the height of her heroic endeavours and at the summit of her glory. Not since the battle at Salamis has Greece achieved such greatness and glory as she has today. (Hadjipateras and Fafalios 1995:157)

Greek communist leader Aris Veloukhiotis also elected to refer to history when in October 1944 he alleged that other political parties had refused to unite in the face of the initial Axis attack: "they shitted on Thermopylae and our three hundred" (Woodhouse 1976:4).[7]

For unity was not to last, either within the ranks of the Greeks or between Greece and Britain. British sources faced a challenge in fitting a people who had been simplistically promoted as friends of liberty, democracy, and of Britain, into an increasingly complex political situation. The majority of armed resistance groups in wartime Greece were affiliated to the communists. ELAS, the "National Popular Liberation Army", was established in 1942, though communism itself had arrived in Greece much earlier. Comparatively greater material aid was given by the Allies to the band of *andartes* under Zervas, which positioned itself as anti-communist (Mazower 2001:141, 314). But the British government conceded that supporting the communists too was unavoidable, because ELAS was "militarily the best force available" for resisting the Axis (Woodhouse 1976:42). It was, however, clear to British ministers that although their aims might converge with those of the communists whilst Greece was still under Nazi occupation, the post-war agenda would be somewhat different. The eventual outcome desired by the British was "an independent and non-communist state ruled as a parliamentary democracy" (Alexander, G. M. 1982:245). Thus, "ELAS was seen as a communist-led movement with whom coexistence in peacetime was likely to prove impossible" (Mazower 2001:331). It is evident from first-hand accounts that even before the Germans were ejected from Greece the relationship between partisans and the Allies had deteriorated to the extent that British liaison officers in the field were greeted with apathy and outright hostility (Myers 1985; Ponder 1997).

In retrospect, doubt has been cast upon the extent and nature of the threat that the communists posed to Greece. Their eventual aim was a dictatorship, but many within the party's leadership conceded that, at least initially, their people's democracy would have to take a parliamentary form (Woodhouse 1976:41). It had become apparent that assistance for a revolution in Greece was not forthcoming from Russia, where Stalin had agreed to Churchill's proposal that Greece remain in the British sphere of influence (Woodhouse 1976:180-2). Many members of ELAS were not even communists, still less in favour of Greece becoming a Russian satellite. They had other motives for joining up.

> Patriotism, despair, a sense of humiliation, an awareness that the guerilla's life was preferable to starvation in the occupied towns, or simply a lack of any other way of life. (Woodhouse 1976:27)

Crucially, however, Winston Churchill seems to have been in no doubt that violence on the streets of Athens in December 1944 represented an attempted coup (Mazower 2001:352).

In short order, the British government had had to shape its reaction to the right-wing 1930s dictatorship of Metaxas, and now the prospect of a communist state. The response in Britain to these two real or imagined non-democratic Greek regimes shared common features. In her introduction to modern Greece published in 1947 Isobel Hunter separated the character of the people from the political affiliations of their leadership. The Greeks were "intensely democratic", and "put up a stubborn resistance which lasted all through the occupation and was of great advantage to the Allies" (1947:47-8, 50). The way may have been shown by Metaxas saying no to the Italians, but he was firmly stated to have previously "assumed dictatorial powers" (Hunter 1947:47). However, as Neil Macvicar recalled in his account of serving with British forces in Greece in 1944,

> no doubt the Metaxas regime was one we would have preferred not to be associated with, but neither then nor later did we require fellow fighters for freedom to pass examinations in parliamentary democracy. (1990:15)

In the face of an attempted post-war communist takeover, the British government stood by its belief "that the majority of Greeks were devoted to Britain and opposed to authoritarian rule" (Alexander, G. M. 1982:245). In this view, the Greek people had been dominated by a series of regimes—Greek-fascist, German-fascist, communist—which did not represent their true political sentiments. The Greek defiance of the Axis was represented as the fight for freedom by a race of natural democrats. British efforts against communism could be justified by this contention that the "true" Greek desired the creation of a regular democracy. If interpretations of the Civil War of 1946-9 remain in dispute—the British and Americans saving Greece from an attempted communist takeover, or the British and Americans thwarting the genuine popular will—the results are not. "Physical damage to property, livestock and communications . . . was far greater than under the German occupation" and left Greece with an economic mountain to climb (Woodhouse 1976:265-6, 286).

Following the end of the Civil War, aid was received under the Truman Doctrine, designed to keep Greece on the "right" side of the Iron Curtain. A domino effect was feared, with Soviet influence in Greece eventually affecting the West's trade and military access to the Eastern Mediterranean and Middle East, including the Suez Canal. Successive British and American governments aimed to preserve democratic government in Greece, a country characterized by British ministers as an "unstable though friendly power" (Stefanidis 1999:63). Influential observers were convinced of the seriousness of the threat. According to Sir Reginald Leeper, Britain's ambassador to the wartime Greek government, Greece had escaped the clutches of the Kremlin "thanks to the powerful support provided first by her British and then by her American friends" (Leeper 1950:236). But Leeper was clear that communism was an abnormality within Greek politics: "the Greeks really are a freedom-loving people, whereas the Communists must despise freedom, judging by the way they eschew it" (1950:xv). Leeper sought to absolve the Greeks from blame as merely "the victims of the rivalries between the great Powers and there is no sign that Russia will be willing to let go of what she desires to make her prey" (1950:237). Arthur S. Gould Lee, a retired British Air Vice-Marshall, similarly argued that "the people of Greece are united in one desire—to repulse the foreign-inspired menace that threatens to weaken and seize the state" (Gould Lee 1948:22). This ongoing representation of the Greeks as naturally democratic and opposed to communism gave justification to government policies of ensuring that Greece remained linked to the West and not Russia.

However, at the height of the Cold War the US government itself stood accused of supporting a very *un*democratic regime in Greece—the junta that ruled from 1967 to 1974. American writer Herbert Kubly, who returned from Greece shortly before the coup, argued that his country "must share the guilt of democracy's death in the land where it was born."

> By its support of the anti-Communist hysteria of the extreme right-wing faction in the Greek military, the United States helped set the stage for the colonels' success. (Kubly 1970:ix-x)

More recently, left-wing historian Christopher Hitchens concluded that the US had given "encouragement, training and materials to the anti-constitutional forces before the coup, and it became their patron and protector for seven years afterwards" (1997:64). Certainly, the Nixon administration gave very public support by vetoing American government efforts to withdraw military aid from Greece, and by allowing a US fleet to call at Athens in 1972 (O'Malley and Craig 1999:137).

It was during the time of the colonels that events in another part of the Greek world—Cyprus—reached their worst crisis point. For Britain and America the sovereignty of Cyprus was an extension of the Cold War struggle for Greece. The island was said by one British foreign minister to be strategically important "to Britain and indeed to the free world" (Stefanidis 1999:29). Once Britain had lost permission for its military presence in Egypt, the bases on Cyprus were seen as "the only guaranteed means of protecting Britain's position in the Middle East and the Persian Gulf" (O'Malley and Craig 1999:5-6). I noted in chapter one that attempts were made by Western officials and intellectuals to justify the British refusal of the union of Greece and Cyprus by positing the existence of a separate Cypriot people. Yet it was simultaneously argued that the ordinary Cypriots shared certain characteristics with their mainland cousins, including a hatred of communism. The assistant secretary at the US State Department, General Bedell Smith, told British officials that he did not believe the Cypriots would vote to become communist (Stefanidis 1999:193). Sir Harry Luke, one-time member of the British administration in Cyprus, tried to separate the ordinary people from extremism: "the shrill, irresponsible yapping of indoctrinated bomb-throwing urban adolescents was not the authentic voice of a race of God-fearing farmers and shepherds" (Luke 1965:173). But both British and American governments feared local communists taking power by force. In the late 1940s the Americans had attempted to persuade the Athens government to openly support anti-communist candidates in Cypriot elections, and by the 1960s the CIA was funding those who were conducting "anti-communist warfare" on the island (Stefanidis 1999:6). By the early 1970s Cyprus was considered vital for monitoring Soviet nuclear missile tests, as an early-

warning station for Russian attacks, and as a site from which to respond to
Middle Eastern threats. The US administration regarded the president,
Archbishop Makarios, as a communist sympathiser and "did not want a
Cypriot leader who had leanings towards neutrality or might gravitate
towards Moscow" (Birand 1985:26). A number of recent observers have
suggested that the US colluded in the Greek junta's 1974 invasion of
Cyprus to oust Makarios (Birand 1985:5; Close 2002:133-4; Hitchens
1997:79-80; O'Malley and Craig 1999:152). The British foreign secretary
of the time has been accused by Turkish journalist M. A. Birand of
"washing his hands of the Cyprus affair" (1985:6-7).

British interpretations of the actions of the Greeks in the Second World
War, as well as of the subsequent struggle against communism, affected
the representation of the people within post-war travel writing about
Greece. Many evidently felt that reports from wartime Greece had led
them to a new understanding of the Greeks. Derek Patmore wrote that "the
modern Greek has proved himself an inspiration to all freedom-loving
peoples throughout the world" (Patmore 1943:9). Major-General H.
Rowan-Robinson observed that "the world had resounded with the tale of
their valour" (Rowan-Robinson [1942?]:195). Some concluded that
Greeks could now be recognized simultaneously as the heirs of ancient
Greece and as the inhabitants of a modern country worthy of respect.

> All the free countries owe a great debt to modern Greece. Up until now,
> Greece was considered a small country in terms of wealth and population.
> Today, thanks to her bravery and virtue, she deserves to be recognised as a
> great power . . . No other page in Greece's glorious history honours the
> Greek name more. (*The Daily Telegraph*: Hadjipateras and Fafalios
> 1995:157)

As I show in chapter four the Greeks were represented positively within
post-war travel texts, and specifically as brave, friendly, and hospitable—
qualities which had been consistently emphasised in reports of their
wartime behaviour. The view of the Greek people as democratic by nature,
also a feature of travel writing, reflected the British government's
favoured interpretation of both the Civil and Cold Wars. Writers could not
ignore the differences between Greek attitudes and standards and those
seen in contemporary Britain. But these were dismissed as superficial, not
detracting from the special friendship and affinity felt by the Greeks
towards the British people they encountered—in war or peace.

The historian Norman Davies has recently argued that Greece was "considerably more distant from those of Western Europe than several countries who found themselves on the wrong side of the Iron Curtain" (Davies 1997:28). Nevertheless, as I have outlined in this chapter, Britain and the USA sought to politically attach Greece to "the West" in the immediate post-war period, through American economic aid and the installation of a "democratic" regime at the expense of communism (Davies 1997:1063). This was but the latest chapter in a long history of attempts to intellectually separate the Greeks from the "East". Such efforts had been encouraged by the Greek intelligentsia of the early 1800s to promote the project of independence, and by fledgling Greek governments to forge a distinct national identity. Later, during the Second World War, the British public had been encouraged to feel closer to their wartime allies by viewing them as the descendants of the ancient Greeks, with whom it was believed that they would be more familiar. The modern Greeks were seen as having preserved the essential characteristics of their ancient forebears (democratic, freedom-loving, cultured, and so on), qualities which had also been inherited and were shared by contemporary Britons. Classical comparison was continued by travel writers of the mid-twentieth century in order to understand and interpret the appearance and characteristics of the Greeks they encountered. In peace as in war, the representation of the modern Greeks had been created by collapsing the differences between two modern societies, and between past and present.

CHAPTER THREE

THE SITES AND MONUMENTS OF GREECE
IN BRITISH TRAVEL WRITING

I share the view of William Curtis that

> looking at a ruin is not a neutral exercise. A ruin is something of an open
> text into which one projects the meanings which one wishes to project.
> One sees, to a degree, what one wants to see. (Curtis 1997:2)

In this chapter I reveal the meanings of ruins according to those who
committed their travels in Greece to print in the years following the
Second World War. The way in which ancient Greece was promoted via
the British education system and ancient histories was hugely influential in
producing descriptions of remarkable consistency from travel writers
spanning several decades. I focus upon ten major locations, ranging from
the iconic (the Parthenon) to what we might term the cheerfully neglected
(Sparta). First, however, I outline the various attributes which I considered
when analysing writers' representations of sites in Greece. The results of
my analysis can be found in numerical form as tables 1-4.

Travel as an exercise in the aesthetic appreciation of locations was, of
course, a long-established idea by the middle of the twentieth century.
From at least the late 1700s "travel came to be justified, not scientifically,
but through connoisseurship, first of buildings and works of art and later
of landscapes" (Crawshaw and Urry 1997:181). Certain sites in Greece—
especially the Temple of Poseidon at Sounion—were visited primarily for
their aesthetic attraction, rather than as the location of any particular
historical events (see my categories A-C in tables 1-4). It is clear that there
was an undefined (and indefinable) level of ruination which was
considered acceptable to the viewer. Eric and Barbara Whelpton were
emphatic that use of knowledge or the imagination was no substitute for
physical presence: "many things that excite archaeologists are to us merely
battered stones half buried in the barren earth" (Whelpton and Whelpton
1961:14). However, extensive reconstruction did not receive universal

praise either (D-F). Whilst Stephen Toulmin failed to find value in fragmentary remains—"nothing remained but a jumble of stones" on Santorini—he objected to the over-restoration of Knossos as inauthentic in its appearance (1963:113, 114). Robert Liddell similarly dismissed Thera as "a uniform muddle", but described the more substantial remains of Knossos as "all Sir Arthur Evans' own work" (1954:16, 166). As at Sounion, the aesthetic value of some monuments was enhanced by their surroundings. Christopher Kininmonth explicitly argued that the value of ruins lay "as much in their situations as their architectural form" (1949:134).

But, ultimately, the appreciation of ruins was diminished without an awareness of history, as Lucile and George Brockway explained.

> Greece is a ruggedly beautiful land full of immortally beautiful things; yet these do not exist in a vacuum. The leading reason for travelling to Greece is that so much happened there. All philosophy, Whitehead remarked, is a series of footnotes to Plato. Likewise our arts and letters and sciences—our humanities as well as our ways of waging war and organising peace—all take the forms they do at least in part because of their Greek origins. One travels to Greece, then, in the hope of gaining a better understanding of these origins and hence (more hopefully) a better understanding of ourselves. (Brockway and Brockway 1967:13)

It is clear that sites were found more compelling if something was known about them (L, M, N, P). Ruined walls in Cephallonia were of little interest to Louis Golding (1955:195) because he could unearth no references to them in Homer. In most cases, however, travel writers claimed to be able to identify history on the ground.

> Wherever one travels in Greece the past survives amidst the astonishing landscape; sometimes awakened by a name only, a legend, sometimes still surviving in the relics of archaic and classical architecture. (Powell 1941:109)

Even where there was little to view, a site might still be worth visiting in order to reflect on famous ancient events or to soak up the atmosphere. Colin Simpson enjoyed his excursion to the ancient healing centre of Epidaurus, even though "the ruins of the Sanctuary of Asclepius, fragmentary and down to foundation level, are not nearly so interesting as what we know about the place" (1969:145). Objects gave a sense of connection (H), with even sherds of pots representing for Goran Schildt "a magic link with ancient people" (Schildt 1953:153). Many writers visited sites less with an expectation of discovery, than a desire to reinforce, or gain new insights into, knowledge of the past they already possessed. Duncan Forbes' motivation was "the desire to tread the soil that Agamemnon trod and to sit in the theatre for which Sophocles wrote" (1970:11). Eric Forbes-Boyd was drawn to the relatively obscure location of Mavromati by Pausanias' account of the ancient Messenian Wars (1964:139-42).

As I have suggested, some struggled to make sense of what they saw (J). Lawrence Durrell gathered ancient potsherds, but was unable to reassemble them (1953:104-5). Robert Bell, who even admitted to having been "disappointed with the Acropolis" on a previous visit, contended that "the fact must be faced that to the average person one set of ruins can be very much like another" (1961:246). Thus, sites could be described as being so confusing as to give neither useful information about ancient life to the casual observer nor aesthetic satisfaction. But, elsewhere, Herbert Kubly explored an ancient city where "marble tables and chairs, mortar stones, bathtubs, household utensils, gave a vivid picture of a vigorous civilization" (1970:71). In addition to providing first-hand evidence for ancient culture, some writers argued for the possibility of a more direct experience of the past. According to Robert Payne, the visitor to Greece

> will see the gods and heroes walking in the sky, stepping lightly over mountains, and he will find himself remembering the details of battles in which he fought thousands of years ago. Time will vanish . . . in the dead of night he will hear the ancient ceremonies. (Payne 1965:1)

The claim of "transportation to the past" (H) has been been found by Chloe Chard in the writings of earlier travellers in Europe. Many of those on the Grand Tour had accessed the past through "efforts of intuitive understanding", demonstrating an ability to "convert historical time into personal time" (Chard 1999:20-1). Roland Barthes argued that a similar effect takes hold of those atop the Eiffel Tower.

> The mind finds itself dreaming of the mutation of the landscape which it has before its eyes; through the astonishment of space, it plunges into the mystery of time, lets itself be affected by a kind of spontaneous anamnesis: it is duration itself which becomes panoramic. (Barthes 1979:11)

At Olympia Colin Simpson imagined himself experiencing a typical day at the games (1969:158-9). Emily Kimbrough was able at Mycenae to "evoke an image of Clytemnestra in the palace above, seeing far away

Agamemnon returning from the siege of Troy" (1965:74). Travel writers were clearly experiencing and perceiving sites in the light of what they imagined life to have been like in ancient times. Sites were more often being read through ancient literature than the evidence provided by archaeology.

Historical objects may also be regarded as having symbolic value. David Lowenthal has observed that ruins serve as illustrations of "the transience of great men and deeds . . . the evanescence of life and the futility of effort" (Lowenthal 1985:173). According to Joseph Braddock, viewing Greece was "bound to stab the reflective man with trite thoughts about Time bearing all its sons away; with rather melancholy forebodings" (1967:127). Specific monuments in Greece acquired particular meanings. The Athenian Acropolis, for example, was seen as symbolic of qualities such as culture and democracy. For some travellers, a visit to the Acropolis was of such significance that they wrote of it in terms redolent of a pilgrimage. S. F. A. Coles compared walking the ancient Sacred Way to an earlier journey he had made from Jerusalem to Bethlehem (1965:75). Derek Patmore explicitly named the Acropolis "the real heart of the city and the place of pilgrimage" (1944:17). The sociologist Dean MacCannell (1976) famously described tourists as pilgrims, and more recent anthropological studies have continued to reveal interesting parallels in aims, behaviour and experiences. As with mid-twentieth century travel writers in Greece, pilgrims are already familiar with the form, function and significance of what they are viewing. The visit to a sacred location is therefore, in Glenn Bowman's terms, "an aid to devotion rather than a necessary part of it" (Bowman 2000:107). The journey allows both sets of travellers "to meditate away from the cares and distractions of their everyday lives on places and moments central to their sense of themselves" (Bowman 2000:107). Reactions to sites are also similar in that "as well as being a literal journey, pilgrimage is a journey of the religious imagination" (McKevitt 2000:78).

It is clear that writers' knowledge and expectations of Greek sites coloured their accounts to a significant degree. In addition to the major sites described in the rest of this chapter, the less visited location of Eleusis is a particularly striking example of this process. Modern Eleusis did not make a positive impression. Most writers would have agreed with Duncan Forbes' characterization as a combination of "a poor and shabby village" and "a huge cement factory [that] belched sulphurous smoke into the blue sky" (Forbes 1970:35). Ancient Eleusis was "reverently walled off from the brash commercialism and industry" (Krippner 1957:145). However, to visit its "scanty" ancient remains was apparently "mere pedantry" (Whelpton and Whelpton 1961:49). Such comments about a physical barrier and poorly-understood ruins reflect travel writers' intellectual frustration. The ancient religious ceremonies known as the Mysteries which drew modern travellers to Eleusis were, as their name suggests, equally impenetrable. At some other sites, compensation for the sparseness of ruins could be discovered in ancient texts. At Thebes, for example, it was felt that "the solemnity of beholding this cradle of mighty legends overcame the sordid present" (Mackenzie 1960:43). Emily Kimbrough's account of Thebes concentrated less on the modern reality than her "inner exultance in being able to say to oneself, 'I'm in Thebes,' remembering stories of that powerful and rich city where Oedipus once was king" (Kimbrough 1957:120). Eleusis, however, had become, in the phrase of Colin Simpson (1969:122), a "dull place". With little to see, and even less known, interest was elusive. At Eleusis, "the mystery is gone" (Liddell 1958:13).

In this chapter I look first at four locations to which values were attached according to their roles in ancient history and literature. Delphi was endowed with a sense of mystery and drama, the result not merely of its stunning natural scenery but of travellers' knowledge of historical events which took place there. Mycenae also had a dramatic setting, but the oppressive atmosphere described by visitors was heightened by their awareness of the bloody myths with which it was associated. At Olympia, it was the peaceful atmosphere which was emphasised in travel accounts, in remembrance that this was the home of the Olympic Games where harmony and fair play triumphed. Depending upon their length of stay and level of interest, travel writers who visited Crete could visit a number of sites or merely Knossos. The peripheral locations could be seen to have various values, whereas the viewing of Knossos itself was affected by knowledge of the Minotaur myth. Following these locations, I turn my attention to four sites which were admired primarily for their aesthetic qualities. Bassae in the Peloponnese had few historical associations and its importance lay in the temple's architecture and the backdrop. On the island of Aegina, the temple of Aphaia was likewise virtually unknown as a site of historical significance, but its design had found an important place in narratives of architectural development. Corinth was an important city in ancient times, but the nature of the visible remains was such that modern visitors concentrated upon the overall effect of the ruins in the landscape rather than lavishing praise upon the details. Sounion, not far from Athens, had acquired interest through a relatively recent celebrity visitor—Lord Byron—but was, again, primarily a location of aesthetic importance. The final section of this chapter is the story of two cities, viewed very differently by twentieth century travel writers. Athens has a number of archaeological attractions, with the Acropolis afforded the status of the pinnacle of Greek (and Western) civilization. At Sparta, there was undoubtedly less to see, but the lack of enthusiasm mustered by travellers also has much to do with the contemporary views of its ancient past which I described in the previous chapter.

(i) Myths and History: Delphi, Mycenae, Olympia, Crete

Included in 43% of accounts, Delphi was, after the Athenian Acropolis, the site most frequently discussed by travel writers during the mid-twentieth century. The belief in Delphi as of central importance to ancient Greece is demonstrated by the inclusion of historical detail within 78% of descriptions. The story of the oracle was commonly outlined, including discussion of how it functioned and the pronouncement issued to Croesus of Lydia that his attack on Persia would lead to the fall of a mighty empire (his own, it transpired). The momentous nature of ancient events here was reflected in the portrayal of the site, particularly the mountain scenery, as dramatic in 70% of the descriptions. For John Pollard, as for others, it was

> not the temple ruins that take one's breath away, but the solemn majesty of the cliffs, and the eagles, the living symbols of ancient deity, wheeling about their flanks. (Pollard 1955:54)

The ancient remains had become merely aesthetic highlights on a larger canvas. The circular building known as the Tholos was by Robert Liddell's time

> regarded as an ornament to the landscape, [and] is now perhaps more beautiful than at any other time; in ancient times it was hedged in by a huddled confusion of other buildings. (Liddell 1965:74)

The treasury built by the Athenians had "become a focal point for photographs of Delphi, and, both on the spot and in memory, is apt to assume much more than its proper importance" (Liddell 1965:79). Both Kanelli and Vyvyan emphasised the unity of natural and man-made elements. These were "stones that rise with the rocks of the background precipice; delicate blocks that have grown out of the earth from eternity to eternity" (Kanelli 1965:184); and every fragment "seemed to belong to that place as surely as if it were rooted in the soil" (Vyvyan 1955:83).

The combination of the scenery and the knowledge which writers brought with them had a powerful effect (G). Some simply felt "awed" (Liddell 1965; Pollard 1955), whilst others experienced an "atmosphere of mystery and living antiquity" (Krippner 1957:141), or were left "spiritually rather overpowered" (Warner 1950:97). For Robert Payne, Delphi was "still a place of religious terror" (Payne 1961:100), and Clara Vyvyan found herself whispering, as though "treading on holy ground" (Vyvyan 1955:83). The site possessed a vestigial, elemental power, deriving from man, nature and the gods. In such a situation, the boundaries between past and present seemed to dissolve. Barbara Whelpton wrote of visitors interpreting echoing voices as "the voice of Apollo calling back to them", and feeling that if they returned at night they "would find nymphs dancing among the broken pillars and sanctuaries of the ancient gods" (Whelpton 1954:103). More prosaically, Delphi could also be regarded as embodying the whole Greek travel experience: "mountains, a view of the sea, temples and pastoral solitude" (Schildt 1953:130).

Mycenae was the third most popular site for comment by travel writers of the period, described within 39% of their accounts. Eric Forbes-Boyd found himself visiting with "the fervour of a pilgrim approaching a shrine" (1964:60). Mycenae offered Rex Warner a unique window upon "the most ancient civilisation in Europe" (1950:115). As a leading classicist, Warner might be expected to align himself with recent scholarly research which, as we saw in chapter one, had revised Schliemann's wilder claims for the site. But, to many, the remains of Mycenae lacked interest if they were to be viewed merely for their archaeological information. Mycenae seemed "very ancient and ruinous" and thus "confusing" to Duncan Forbes (1970:52). Few travel writers—just 17%—expressed appreciation for the aesthetics of the excavated structures, though the striking situation garnered more praise, Patrick Anderson finding "a landscape of exquisite rightness" (1963:152). But the site came alive once travellers began to recall the stories of the ill-fated family of Agamemnon. Despite the severance of the direct link between Agamemnon and Schliemann's finds, this remained "territory famed in history, legend and drama" (Coles 1965:93). The vast majority of travel writers—69%—chose to recount at least part of the myths for their readers. Nancy Spain admitted to having recently attended a performance of Euripides' *Electra*, which explained her becoming "terribly over-excited by the postern gate and the bath and the tomb, and the barren hills and the brooding landscape that must have driven the whole Elektra family dotty" (1964:202).

These elements of landscape, a bloody legend, and anticipation, together created imaginings of an oppressive and menacing atmosphere. Charmian Clift found "a sombre, brooding place, impregnated with blood and darkness, and a lingering echo of life" (1958:156). Lawrence Durrell fled from Mycenae "with its burial grounds choked with bodies, and the obsessive numbing drone of bees in the dark tomb of Agamemnon" (1945:72). Tiryns, a city of the same period, received much less attention, and its reception illustrates the extent to which knowledge of myth affected those visiting Mycenae. Tiryns gave "nothing like the impression of strength and grandeur one gets at Mycenae" (Forbes 1970:57), and Emily Kimbrough found that "curiously, although the ruins of Tiryns are better preserved than those at Mycenae, to us they were nowhere near so dramatic" (1957:151). Rex Warner was sufficiently self-analytical to realise that "one's memories of the bloody legend of the house of Atreus will affect one's sensations when one is standing on the ground where one may imagine Orestes to have stood" (1950:118).

Olympia was described in almost one-third (29%) of travel texts. Robert Payne described it as "the most sacred place on earth", because in his view the Olympic Games provided the "impetus" for Greek civilization (1961:42-3). Travel writers commonly thought of the games as civilizing occasions which promoted harmony between ancient city-states and demanded outstanding virtues of competitors. Such wholesome qualities were transcribed onto the site which travellers visited in the mid-twentieth century. The peaceful valley (B) and details of the historical background (P) were equally frequent topics within travel writing (both at 59%). For Goran Schildt, Olympia's landscape invited "tranquil meditation" and the archaeological remains had the "air of a deserted churchyard" (1953:118). Payne emphasised how the rolling hills seemed feminine in comparison to the masculinity of Delphi (1961:42). Derek Patmore found that

> like so many other historic places in Greece, it is the associations and memories which give Olympia its quality rather than the ruins and relics which one can still see there. (1944:33)

The calmness of Olympia allowed some writers to indulge in these "associations" and roll away the present. Eric Forbes-Boyd was left with "the impression that this is still a sanctuary, and you an intruder on the mysteries" (1964:206).

The various sites of the Minoan culture to be found on Crete were described by travel writers as offering very different viewing experiences. Schildt felt it was beneficial to have the opportunity of visiting an "unspoiled ruin" in addition to the "reconstruction" that was Knossos (1953:286). But Dilys Powell found sites such as Mallia confusing: "at Knossos with Evans's restorations one at any rate knew where one was" (1973:20). There was considerable debate amongst travellers about whether Sir Arthur Evans' physical reconstruction of Knossos revealed or obscured the truth. Christopher Kininmonth praised Evans' work, for "while he has not obliterated the quality peculiar to a ruined site, he has enabled one to bring it vividly to life in one's mind" (1949:179). However, to Monica Krippner the remains of Knossos looked false and she preferred to visit Phaestos, which she could reconstruct in her own imagination (1957:175). Knossos was rendered incomprehensible for Phoebe-Lou Adams by its jumble of different habitation levels: the "traditional connotations of the word labyrinth are inadequate to express the confusion of Daedalean architecture" (1965:67).

As we saw in previous chapters, Evans had sought to uncover the origin of the labyrinth. Travel writers' impressions were in part shaped by Evans' references to the Minotaur and his characterization of the somewhat barbaric culture from which the creature derived. Dilys Powell, some-time resident of Knossos as the wife of archaeologist Humfry Payne, remembered "the pall of history pressing bloodstained and heavy on summer days", and "something sacrificial in the air" (1973:9). Sheelagh Kanelli found "the ghosts of that elegant, cultured, yet disaster-ridden race amongst their bright pillars and paint are pleadingly alive just beyond the borders of existence" (1965:187). In the 1950s the writing of ancient Crete, known as Linear B, was revealed through the work of Michael Ventris to be an early form of Greek. This turned one of Evans' central contentions on its head: rather than the Minoans exporting civilization to the mainland, it appeared as though Crete had been conquered by the Mycenaean Greeks. Nevertheless, as late as the 1960s travel writers continued to portray Knossos as the origin of later Greek civilization. Herbert Kubly, for example, approached Crete with "awe" as "one of the great wombs of civilisation" (1970:102, 104).

(ii) Aesthetics: Bassae, Aegina, Corinth, Sounion

The Temple of Apollo was described within only 14% of travel texts of the mid-twentieth century, giving justification to Derek Patmore's comment that Bassae was "little-visited" (1944:89). Although access for motor vehicles improved in the post-war period, the site remained relatively remote, and writers seem to have become less adventurous as time went on—or felt that their potential readers had become less interested in such a "minor" classical relic. It rated inclusion in 40% of 1940s accounts, compared with 7% and 13% in the 1950s and '60s respectively (although it should be noted that fewer texts were published in the 1940s). When travellers did visit, Bassae was regarded as notable for the characteristic which helped to keep visitors away—its isolation. In Colin Simpson's view, the landscape at Bassae "was the one piece of Arcadia I had seen that could be called Arcadian" (1969:224). Eric Forbes-Boyd found this "temple in the wilderness indescribably moving" (1964:197-8). The aesthetics of the ruins against the wild mountain backdrop frequently received praise within descriptions (C). The temple "seemed to be part of the landscape", born "of the mountain" (Kubly 1970:200); which, since it was constructed from local materials, was indeed the case. For J. E. Morpurgo, Bassae was "the finest of all classical sites" (1963:188-9).

Visits to the temple on the island of Aegina near Athens were recorded in only 18% of the travel accounts published in the mid-twentieth century. Most of the writers of these (76%) discussed the history and architecture of the temple, and in particular the identity of the goddess to which it was dedicated: Aphaia was relatively obscure and writers evidently felt the necessity to outline what was known about her. The most important reason for visiting the site was, however, not its role in history, which was insignificant compared with Delphi or Olympia. Robert Payne maintained that there was "little record in history" about the island of Aegina and its temple (1965:156). Rather, the aesthetics of this building were paramount. In particular, it was the combination of ruined temple and imposing coastal view that seemed to strike a number of writers (in 65% of the accounts that mention the site). For Goran Schildt, the temple was "outstanding thanks to its position" (1953:173), and Compton Mackenzie found that it "rivals in the beauty of its site the temple of Poseidon at Sounion" (1960:171; see below). Payne suggested that more could be read into the building than simply developments in ancient architectural style:

to him, the "masculine authority" of the columns reflected the ancient islanders' hardy nature (1961:109).

Corinth was another site relatively neglected by travel writers, described in only 23% of their accounts. In ancient times Corinth was one of the greatest cities on the Greek mainland, but modern travellers have found that the extant remains fail to live up to its former importance, because they are "very largely Roman" (Schildt 1953:166). This overlaying of later buildings on the Greek city was detrimental to mental reconstruction, and there were differing views on whether the modern visitor was able to make sense of what remained. For S. F. A. Coles, Corinth was merely a "scattering of ruins" (1965:36), whereas Leslie Finer characterized the remains as "varied and appealing" (1964:206). Due to the extensively Roman nature of what could be seen in the lower city, travel writing of the mid-century period contained less comment on the aesthetics of the buildings themselves than on the striking location.

> It is not a place that has ever attracted me . . . To my mind time spent among these fallen columns is wasted if it deters one from making the ascent of Acrocorinth itself. All the way up this great hill open up enormous views of sea and mountain. (Warner 1950:112)

The remains of the Temple of Apollo were "grandly impressive, but, like so many temple ruins, they please the 'picturesque traveller' as landscape rather than as architecture" (Liddell 1958:35).

Cape Sounion in Attica was visited, usually as a day trip from Athens, for its temple to Poseidon. The aesthetic qualities of the remains were often commented upon (within 47% of the descriptions). The temple was described as a "gracious ruin" (Golding 1955:102), and "a white and graceful gull" compared to the "gold and massive eagle" of the Parthenon (Pollard 1955:60). The aesthetic effect of the ruin against the realm of Poseidon itself was of some interest (B and C, at 33 and 30% respectively). According to Hazel Thurston, "the chief wonder of this place now lies in its site" (1960:148). This, together with the "lean and athletic appearance" of the columns, made the temple seem "to stand like a diver, stripped, and ready to dive or, since it is divine, to fly into the air" (Warner 1950:141-2). For Emily Kimbrough, the scene "was so beautiful as very nearly to make us weep" (1957:158). The history of the site was outlined within one-third of accounts. Many writers thought a visit was of little value for specific historical associations: no major events took place there in antiquity. In a book otherwise heavy on detail, Robert Payne gave little history on Sounion (1961:129), and for W. A. Wigram it "lacks all human interest" (1947:94-5). However, one modern visitor received some attention, in 40% of texts: Lord Byron, who left his name carved in the stones (e.g. Golding 1955:102-3). Writers hoped to recapture the artistic inspiration he apparently found there.

(iii) Rival Cities: Athens and Sparta

Dilys Powell explained that when compared with Rome, "the temples and theatres of the Acropolis apart, the architectural monuments of classical Athens are, for the unscholarly, not many or inescapable." However, she found that "gradually as one walks about Athens the consciousness of the past grows stronger": through the street names, the dominant Acropolis, and the landscape (Powell 1941:68). Approximately 40% of travel writers of the mid-century period discussed Athenian sites and monuments other than the Acropolis. These additional ancient locations included the Theatre of Dionysus, the Temple of Hephaistus, the Agora, the Cerameicus cemetery, and the Temple of Olympian Zeus. Descriptions of—and values ascribed to—these sites remained largely consistent in travel writing across the thirty year period from the end of the Second World War.

The Theatre of Dionysus was thought to have played a central role in cultural history. As we have seen, Greek myths—many of which were retold by the ancient tragedians—retained a powerful hold over the collective British imagination for much of the twentieth century. This theatre, though rebuilt in antiquity, was "the home and shrine of drama, the very birth-place of comedy and tragedy both" (Wigram 1947:48). For Monica Krippner, the Cerameicus cemetery was an oasis of calm amongst an Athenian suburb otherwise swamped by dirt and noise (1957:21). For perhaps this reason, S. F. A. Coles found it easy to visualize the spot from which Pericles gave his funeral oration for the dead of Athens' war against Sparta (1965:64).[8] In contrast, as a largely Roman edifice the Temple of Olympian Zeus was regarded as of little historical importance. Instead, writers concentrated upon its aesthetics. John Pollard emphasised the "ornate Corinthian capitals, burgeoning whitely against the blue", and the "view through the pillars towards the Acropolis" (1955:22).

At the Agora, the ancient marketplace and centre of administration, "there was not a great deal to see" (Forbes 1970:25) for aesthetic or literary reasons. Coles (1965:38-9) felt himself transported back in time to

witness the Panathenaic procession, conjured from his memories of the
Parthenon frieze in London, as it wound through the Agora on its way to
the Acropolis. The adjacent Temple of Hephaistus—whose surroundings
had been newly landscaped—contrasted favourably with the reconstructed
Stoa of Attalus which "suffers badly from the lack of greenery to break its
stiff facade" (Adams 1965:94). The temple was often described as "well-
preserved" (e.g. Anderson 1958:75; Payne 1965:155; Simpson 1969:63),
but it regularly failed to impress. Osbert Lancaster went so far as to call it
"devastatingly boring" (1947:48). The reputation of the Hephaisteion
suffered from being within sight of a more illustrious temple of the fifth
century BC, the Parthenon. In addition, unlike the Agora itself, the
Hephaisteion had no compensatory historical interest. As I noted earlier,
even the name of this temple—formerly known as the Theseum—had
been in dispute until earlier in the twentieth century.

The Acropolis was the site most regularly included in travel books on
Greece published between 1940 and the early 1970s. Most writers (73%)
commented on the aesthetics of the principal remains themselves—of the
Parthenon, Erechtheion, Propyleia, and Temple of Athena Nike. The latter
received universal praise: "graceful" (Whelpton and Whelpton 1961:32)
and "a flawless diamond on a band of gold" (Smith, Ashley 1948:198).
The Erechtheion had a more mixed reception: either the second most
impressive building of antiquity (Whelpton and Whelpton 1961:31), or as
"curious rather than beautiful" (Pollard 1955:18). The Parthenon itself was
acclaimed as "the most beautiful building in the world" (Braddock
1967:166). Its ruined state had little effect on its aesthetics: it was able to
"lose all its decoration and be smashed to pieces beside, and yet remain a
marvel at which the world holds its breath" (Wigram 1947:27).

Many writers of Acropolis accounts (55%) praised the aesthetic effects
of these monuments in conjunction with the surrounding rock. The
Parthenon's "clear and majestic outlines" emerged from "its white hill"
(Coles 1965:31, 37). However, some were critical about the imposition of
modernity upon their viewing experience. Betty Roland was disappointed
to discover that new buildings blocked the view from the city of the
"unbelievable perfection" of the ancient monuments (1963:3). The
Acropolis was now "in the middle of a sprawling urbanization of
landscape" (Braddock 1967:155), so that the visitor looked out across an
"ugly, smoky little city" (Andrews 1959:216; for similar observations:
Golding 1955:16; Pollard 1955:22; Smith, Ashley 1948:36; Vyvyan
1955:33, 34). These sentiments are comparable to the representation of the

city found by Penny Travlou during her examination of guidebooks to Athens.

> There are two different time narratives within the same space; one refers to classical Athens and the other to the modern city. These narratives show a preference and therefore resurrection of the former and a sort of indignation towards the qualities of the latter. (Travlou 2002:111)

But the Acropolis still allowed Patrick Anderson the "whole Greek experience", as he could take in through "the hazy view my special subsidiary places" (1958:206; i.e. the Plaka, Tower of the Winds, Lysicrates' monument, the Temple of Olympian Zeus and Hadrian's Arch). Roland Barthes explained in an essay how another iconic structure—the Eiffel Tower—becomes an intellectual as well as a physical vantage point: "to visit the Tower is to get oneself up onto the balcony in order to perceive, comprehend, and savor a certain essence of Paris" (Barthes 1979:8). Barthes went on to emphasise the creative nature of such a viewing, with the individual's mind constructing their own geography of the city based on their previous knowledge (1979:9-10). Likewise, from the Acropolis, Anderson picked out the other landmarks with which he was most familiar and interested.

Relatively few accounts of the Acropolis monuments (41%) included specific details about their past—dates, builders, role in history, and so on. A number of writers explained this omission as due to familiarity. The Acropolis was "universally known" (Thurston 1960:135), and the Parthenon "something we had seen for many years in pictures and in day-dreams" (Vyvyan 1955:33). Eric and Barbara Whelpton assumed that, although they had outlined the ancient and modern history of the Parthenon, the reader would not need a description of its modern appearance, "which everyone has seen in models and photographs from their earliest years" (1961:31). In part, descriptions of the Acropolis monuments lacked substance because the heart of the Parthenon was missing. What writers regarded as the most important artistic legacy of the ancient world—the Parthenon frieze, metopes, and pedimental sculptures, otherwise known as the "Elgin Marbles"—resided under grey skies and grey stone in London, not in warm Athenian sunshine. The detailed history of what remained in situ was less important than the monuments' aesthetics, because although the Acropolis was at the centre of the city, the scenes of ancient battles, debates and philosophy were elsewhere. Thus, in comparison to other sites in Greece, very few writers experienced imaginative time travel on the Acropolis.

The Parthenon—and by extension the entire building complex—was elevated (or reduced) by travel writers to a symbol. The sociologist John Urry has noted that "as tourists we see objects which are constituted as signs. They stand for something else" (1990:129). Roland Barthes discussed this phenomenon in relation to the Eiffel Tower. As "a universal symbol of Paris", the tower was "the major sign of a people and a place" (Barthes 1979:3-4). Visitors came to the tower "to participate in a dream of which it is . . . much more the crystallizer than the true object" (Barthes 1979:7). For travel writers in Athens, the Acropolis / Parthenon was, firstly, a symbol of Athenian culture and history. As I showed in the previous chapter, this was often thought to be synonymous with ancient Greek culture and history as a whole.

> The whole edifice is charged with a vitality that transcends time, and it is easy to understand how it has come to symbolize for the modern world everything that is denoted by the term "classic". (Pollard 1955:16)

Rex Warner added: "not that the unity and the extent in time and space of Greece is *wholly* symbolised by a rock in Athens or by Athens itself" (1950:27, my emphasis). Derek Patmore explored at length how it was that at the Acropolis "you came to realize and appreciate the spirit of Hellenic civilization and the beauty of Greek art" (1944:17). He found it "encouraging to remember that these buildings and ruins have withstood the assault of time", so that "everlasting and indestructible, Ancient Greece lives on" (1944:18).

As I discussed in chapter two, for many Greeks of modern times the ruinous state of the Acropolis has symbolised the country's "losses and its aspirations for regeneration", so that "the restoration works on the Acropolis could thus be seen as a metonymy for the Greek nation's efforts to restore its ancient glory" (Yalouri 2001:185). Some British travel writers, including Barbara Whelpton, picked up on this association.

> Built over and made to look like a Turkish city . . . it remained in this state until . . . [the Greeks] were able to free their country from foreign rule . . . Then began the great work of restoring the Acropolis to something of its former glory. (Whelpton 1954:85)

S. F. A. Coles viewed the Parthenon as important "because of its compelling loveliness and majesty, and the thirty centuries of history that it embodies and personifies" (1965:44).

In addition, the Acropolis could be regarded as symbolic of Western culture as a whole, as Evan John's account shows.

> The few square miles of city, hill and plain visible from its summit had once bred . . . men who have led and taught the whole world in all those matters . . . on which modern civilisation rests. (John 1954:127)

Emily Kimbrough's encounter with the Acropolis led to similar reflections—and reduced her to tears.

> This is the crown of the whole Western world. Every single one of us lives under this and because of this. This is where we've got our way of life, democracy, human relations, political patterns, sculpture, literature, theater. Why, this is coming back to where I came from. This is home, my home, the home of everybody in the world I know about. (Kimbrough 1957:66)

More generally, the Acropolis was a symbol of human achievement. The buildings were "the inspired architectural expression of man's affinity with and adoration of his natural environment" (Finer 1964:183). As a result, "there is nowhere else in the world a worthier monument to mankind than on these few acres of bare stone" (Smith, Ashley 1948:210). As Mary Beard has recently noted, "the Parthenon, as one of the acknowledged masterpieces of fifth-century culture, can stand as a visible guarantee of the virtues of democracy", both ancient and modern (Beard 2002:118). The identification of the Parthenon as a symbol of culture and democracy is aided by the sculptural elements of the building (or the metopes at least), which showed mythical scenes of Greeks triumphing over centaurs—civilization versus barbarism (Beard 2002:144).

I suggested earlier that travel to Greece was described by some writers in terms of a pilgrimage. Nowhere is this more noticeable than in accounts of the Acropolis. "That first glimpse of the Parthenon is surely one of the great and unforgettable experiences in life and for such a moment I had travelled all those long sea miles." (Roland 1963:3) A visit to "the most sacred spot that pre-Christian Europe has left us" (John 1954:127), might be "a life experience more than an impression" (Coles 1965:196). After all, to this generation, the Parthenon was the "most famous building in the Western world" (Simpson 1969:1).

From mid-twentieth century travel literature it is clear that the city of Sparta had lost the popularity battle to its ancient rival Athens. Just 15% of texts included a visit. Sparta's remains were said to be "difficult to find" (Kubly 1970:196), and Barbara Whelpton decided to stay away because "there's not very much left to see" (1954:115). Several writers showed that they knew their Thucydides by relating the prophecy, contained in his history of the Peloponnesian War, that Sparta would leave little visible after her demise (Andrews 1959:176; Coles 1965:127-8; Mackenzie 1960:188).[9] Though few went so far as to suggest that they were ugly (just three in fact), this was, strikingly, a set of remains whose aesthetics were not praised by a single writer.

The absence of remains found at Sparta—and the absence of visits compared with Athens—reflects the contemporary view I outlined in the previous chapter that, despite their comparable power in ancient times, Sparta was the less significant of the two cities in terms of its cultural legacy to the Western world. Travel writers believed that the Spartan character could be read in the stones. In Monica Krippner's view, the dull and lifeless ruins seemed a reflection of an ancient over-preoccupation with militarism (1957:184). For Robert Liddell, Sparta had "a lovely but uneasy landscape, and it fills one with love and thankfulness for the calm classical beauty of Attica" (1958:149). Liddell explicitly mapped his own negative views of ancient Sparta on to her extant remains: "for once it is gratifying to see an ancient city in ruins", as "the very name of Sparta is hateful: this, the only totalitarian state in ancient Greece" (1958:132, 135). Similarly, Colin Simpson, who regarded the ancient city as producing "a warrior society that was essentially destructive and backward and incapable of change", maintained that "the good thing about going to Sparta is finding it gone" (Simpson 1969:226).

These reactions to ancient Sparta and its material remains reveal some very twentieth century concerns about ways of running a state.

Poor Sparta! Neither its architecture nor its ancient values are much in fashion now. Lycurgus, once regarded as a great law-maker, appears now, to our mid-twentieth-century minds, as some monstrous despot of a police state. He it was who, perhaps first in history, realized the value of catching his soldiers young. His whole educational system was devoted to the subjugation of the individual to the state. Discipline and endurance, these were the qualities that mattered. No dictator of modern times has gone quite so far in his efforts to achieve a race of supermen. (Osler 1957:127)

Michael Osler's vision of Sparta—with its emphasis on the attempt to create a superior race—reflects the correlation I discussed earlier between

Germany-Sparta-dictatorship and Britain-Athens-democracy. Colin Simpson more explicitly compared the system of the Spartans—"a people who were brain-washed from infancy by a totalitarian State"—to Nazi Germany (1969:231-3). John Pollard viewed Sparta as more Soviet than Fascist: "the most efficient system of military communism that the world has ever known." The city had an "ancient equivalent of the Russian OGPU" to keep internal security. Yet she was incapable of holding together an empire since "like most totalitarian states she found it easy to discipline her citizens only when they remained at home." Once away from Sparta, the lure of the outside world proved too attractive to those used to severity, and lifestyles lapsed (Pollard 1955:99, 100). As we saw previously, in Britain—though not in Nazi Germany—the military regime of Sparta was seen unfavourably as the antithesis of Athens. The democracy of Athens, whilst itself possessing an empire, had sponsored a flowering of culture. This view of history provided models, precedents, and justification, for the British Empire, at a time when its existence was under threat, as well as a reading of the 1939-45 conflict.

John Urry has noted that to be the focus of a tourist's attention, "there must be certain aspects of the place to be visited which distinguish it from what is conventionally encountered in everyday life" (1990:11). As we have seen, travel writers have often regarded a visit to Greece as more than simply a holiday. Ancient Greece was central to their own cultural identity as twentieth century Britons. A number of travel writers nevertheless demonstrated a degree of awareness that the primacy of classics was being challenged at home, and that the nature and purpose of travel to Greece was undergoing change. In his book *Greece: The Unclouded Eye*, Colin Simpson observed that the 1967 slogan of the Greek Tourist Organization—"You were born in Greece"—had, the following year, been transformed into "Fun in Greece" (Simpson 1969:38). For Simpson, this illustrated that "more potential Greece-goers wanted fun-with-sun than wanted to listen to the Greek stones speak of cultural heritage" (1969:38). Authors and publishers of travel books began to consider that their potential readers may no longer regard themselves as "pilgrims" to the sites and monuments. For example, travel writers of the 1960s were burdening their readers with less historical information than those of the previous decade. As can be seen in tables two and three, category P becomes a less significant topical domain in the descriptions of seven of the ten major sites I have discussed in this chapter. At the beginning of the 1960s, Robert Bell was arguing that although "in the past it appealed mainly to the archaeologist, the classical scholar and the keen student",

Greece "is now making strenuous efforts to attract the ordinary visitor" (1961:16). Hence, in his book, Bell habitually gave only the briefest of information on sites he encountered: Eleusis was "where ancient religious rites known as Eleussion mysteries were celebrated; here we turned left" (Bell 1961:247). At the same time, Bell used his account as an attempt to convince readers of the enduring legacy of the ancient Greek achievement.

> Modern science and the West's distinctive way of life—its basic values of freedom of the mind, originality, and the importance of the individual—are a continuance and unfolding of Greek science and culture and would not exist without it. (Bell 1961:106)

In the 1990s visitors, still, of course, sought out the ancient sites of Greece. But the balance of motives had undergone a transformation since those professed and witnessed by travel writers during the middle of the century. Jennifer Craik divided 1990s visitors into three groups.

> Only a minority of tourists are truly cultural tourists (of the Grand Tour type) while a significant number are "culture proof". Of those in the middle, many tourists may be motivated to take advantage of cultural attractions once other, primary motivations to travel have been met. (Craik 1997:120)

For many writers during the middle decades of the twentieth century, however, interest in the past was the unquestioned primary motive for travel in Greece. In their accounts, the characterization of each of the country's major sites was influenced by earlier travel literature, popular histories, and the high status classics had been afforded within formal education. The legacy of Greece may no longer have been universally venerated as it had once been, but the status and representation of its monuments remained remarkably consistent.

CHAPTER FOUR

THE GREEK PEOPLE IN BRITISH TRAVEL WRITING

In his travel book of the late 1960s Colin Simpson explained that he had nothing against the "simple pleasures" of sun and sea. But, for him, the "reward of the stones is quite another matter" (1969:39). Other writers, however, were much less interested in visiting Greece's dusty and confusing past, and paid more attention to their encounters with local people. C. P. Lee dismissed ruins and monuments from his account altogether, in favour of aiding the West's understanding of "Greeks very much alive today, how and what they think, how and what they eat, how and what they have done, do, and would like to do" (1957:17). Even where writers lacked this explicit focus, they invariably observed appearance or behaviour in passing. Such brief comments are equally important when assessing the common features of the representation of the Greeks within travel accounts. In this chapter I focus on the three main themes of this representation. Firstly, I argue that, consciously or unconsciously, many travel writers compared the Greeks with the ancient people of that name. Sometimes this was deliberate, part of a strategy to encourage readers to believe that the Greeks were a people with whom they were already familiar. At other times the process was more subtle: travel writers endowed the Greeks with characteristics which were commonly associated with the ancient world. I have, for example, argued in previous chapters that the ancient Greeks were thought to have been natural democrats. In mid-twentieth century travel literature this label was, usually unquestioningly, applied to the modern people by a large number of writers. Associated with this is the second strand of this chapter, in which I show that Greece was regularly depicted as a collection of rural and primitive communities, in spite of the rapid expansion of cities such as Athens. This "timelessness" served to portray the Greeks as relics of a bygone age, as a people untainted by progress, but who would also benefit from Western tutelage. At times, however, the perception of a lack of progress tipped over into Orientalism. The Greeks were seen negatively as having acquired the backward, Eastern ways of the Turks, as I describe in the third section. Throughout this chapter, I make my case with reference to a series of characteristics of the Greek people, the prevalence of which I have tracked across travel texts. The numerical results of my analysis can be found in tables 5, 6 and 7 (appendix C).

(i) The Greeks as Classical Relics

As in earlier periods, travellers of the 1940s to '70s claimed almost invariably to have met with a positive reception in Greece. As can be seen in table 5, Greeks were described as "friendly" or "curious" towards their guests in 83% of texts. Some writers went so far as to suggest that "friendliness" was a trait possessed by all Greek people (e.g. Mais and Mais 1962:88; Powell 1941:118; Tremayne 1958:13; Vyvyan 1955:42). The existence of a "national curiosity about foreigners" (Vyvyan 1955:103) was also posited. Writers described how they and their companions were routinely interrogated about such personal matters as wealth, marital status, children, relationships with each other, and reasons for travelling in Greece. In Patrick Leigh Fermor's view, this "eager questioning of visitors" was a combination of desire to "establish common ground" and a "thirst for knowledge" (Leigh Fermor 1958:205). Emily Kimbrough thought of the Greek's curiosity as a deliberate effort to show interest, "another expression of his [sic] hospitality"; whilst C. P. Lee suggested that locals found background information about strangers useful when discussion inevitably turned to weightier matters such as politics (Kimbrough 1965:135; Lee, C. P. 1957:18).

The presence of these features of Greek behaviour was, of course, to some extent dependent upon the area and decade in which the writer was travelling. For example, Xan Fielding regularly encountered villages where people rarely saw an outsider: he claimed to be one of only two Englishmen in Crete at the time (1953:173). Strangers in more touristic areas such as Athens would hardly arouse the same surprise among the inhabitants. But, as table 6 shows, an overwhelming majority of the texts published during each of the three decades following the Second World War included examples of Greeks exhibiting curiosity or friendliness. For a substantial minority of writers (37%) this was a significant aspect of Greek behaviour, in that they referred to it five or more times (table 7). One effect of this portrayal was to underscore the differences from the British. Greeks lived their lives free from the hypocrisy and cynicism so common in Britain, something which might change with the advent of mass tourism and the increasing influence of Western European culture (see below). On Cyprus, the villagers whom Lawrence Durrell had lived among, previously so friendly and hospitable, grew distant. This, however, was attributable to the actions of the British authorities, who had executed a Greek terrorist demanding *enosis* (Durrell, L. 1957:247-9). Overall, *unfriendly* Greeks were a very rare occurrence.

The Greeks were commonly (in 87% of accounts) said to express their friendship and interest towards travellers not merely verbally but through acts of generosity and hospitality. There were offers of food, drink, lodging, directions, guiding duties, and so on, usually without the expectation of payment. Some writers built up a picture of being doted upon as they travelled from one community to the next (e.g. Andrews 1959; Fielding 1953; Pollard 1955). In the 1940s, Ashley Smith was treated "in a kingly fashion" on his visit to Missolonghi (1948:152). On most occasions, visitors to monasteries were welcomed with food and drink, and sometimes a bed for the night (e.g. Liddell 1965:176, 183, 188). Duncan Forbes described this as the "traditional courtesy to travellers, which is still extended even to the obvious tripper of today" (1970:147). Many writers explicitly listed generosity and hospitality as features of the national character (e.g. Anderson 1958:67; Durrell, L. 1945:59; Kimbrough 1957:6), an element in the portrayal of a more innocent society, less grasping and materialistic than that of the "West". Some writers, such as Robert Liddell (1965:215), were disparaging of those who travelled with the intention of living on the hospitality of villagers and monks. But Patrick Leigh Fermor argued for the necessity of acceptance, because "hospitality in Greece has an almost religious importance" (Leigh Fermor 1958:204). Liddell recognized it as "a sacred virtue" dating from antiquity (1958:21). Several other writers described Greek hospitality as an example of continuity from the ancient world. Joseph Braddock, for example, maintained that "their hospitality to the foreigner in their midst has been renowned since classical times" (1970:157). Eric Forbes-Boyd looked further back, suggesting that it was "a survival of the old Homeric times" (1964:103).

For a few, this hospitality became burdensome. Robert Liddell admitted that "whoever the guest may be, his hosts are unweariedly, even wearyingly, devoted to him" (1958:21). Despite initial impressions, Xan Fielding discovered that a payment of sorts was required: conversation. "They could never have enough of it . . . Silence was never golden; not a moment for reading or reflection" (Fielding 1953:128-9). Kevin Andrews was expected to use his supposed connections—as an important American, perhaps even an officer or a spy, rather than the scholarship student of reality—to intercede with the authorities on behalf of his hosts, or to procure opportunities for them in Greece or abroad (1959:204ff). Betty Roland warned her readers about what she regarded as the "myth" of "warmheartedness and universal hospitality": wealthier Greeks would only be generous if they viewed the friendship of the recipient as an asset (1963:70). In most cases, however, offers came without apparent strings. Even though she was an avowed *tourist*, Phoebe-Lou Adams found that the hotel manager on Kos charged her just half of the advertised cost for her stay (1965:45ff). Michael Osler experienced "the usual Greek courtesy and kindness", even in Athens (1957:118). However, some writers observed that the increase in the number of visitors was causing attitudes to change. On Skiathos, Nancy Spain noted that "in twelve months the sacred stranger had become the not-so-sacred tourist" (1964:212). By 1970, according to Duncan Forbes, Greeks had become wise to long-haired "beatniks" who attempted to take advantage of them (1970:80). Unwillingness to offer hospitality was thus attributed not to an innate defect in the Greek character, but to the invasion of tourists and the corrupting influence of the West upon a primitive and hitherto unsullied society.

As I explained in chapter two, British wartime propaganda portrayed the Greeks as noble allies who had defied Mussolini and delayed the Axis advance. This had an immediate impact on post-war travel writing, which emphasised Greek courage and fortitude in both peace and war. Over the mid-century period as a whole, 42% of travel texts included references to Greek bravery. When only writing of the 1940s is considered, this rises to 60%. Some writers (e.g. Fielding, Foss, Leigh Fermor) had first-hand experience of Greek resistance exploits as former British agents who had found shelter and aid in the occupied nation. Writing in the very year of the German invasion of Greece, Dilys Powell outlined how "Greeks fought and died for the idea of liberty" (1941:164-5). Following in a long literary tradition, Powell went on to remind readers that in ancient times a similar stand had been taken against the Persians. In the 1960s S. F. A. Coles returned to the theme that the behaviour of the *evzones* in 1940 was like the hoplites at Marathon, representing "the heroic Greek attitude to life and the immemorial stoicism and simplicity of the people" (1965:52-3). To such writers, as for Robert Liddell, ancient and modern fighters "all seem, as they are, part of a single, heroic Greek past" (Liddell 1954:35).

As I have noted previously, through such comparisons and connections, the modern Greeks were rendered familiar to the classically trained reader.

In their narratives of post-war Greece, writers extended the concept of Greek courage to civilian life. John Knowles recorded the rescue of a woman from drowning as a survival of the heroism of the Spartans at Thermopylae (1964:148). In addition, many writers emphasised the courage of the Greeks in the face of their often harsh living conditions. Crossing into Greece from Yugoslavia, Michael Osler found that the people "gave the impression that, if the effort against it proved too great, they would tolerate a certain amount of squalor in their village poverty" (1957:96). The Cretans in particular were usually described as tough (e.g. Mikes 1965:89), but this representation easily tipped over into something less favourable: Greeks as swift to violence. Xan Fielding argued that feuds in Crete meant that the hospitality offered to strangers was not so readily lavished upon the impoverished of their own communities (1953:228-9). Patrick Leigh Fermor contended that the interminable and bloody feuds among the Maniots were undertaken merely for family gain (1958:89-93). For some writers, personal or collected memories of the savagery and pointlessness of the Civil War remained fresh (e.g. Loch 1968:210ff). Sheelagh Kanelli, however, maintained that the majority of Greek men were motivated by a sense of honour, *philotemo* (1965:27-8), for which Joseph Braddock found a classical parallel in Achilles' quarrel with Agamemnon (1970:157-8).

But most Greek people were not regarded as natural killers. Whilst a number of writers recorded incidents of disregard for or cruelty to animals (e.g. Balfour 1951:152; Carroll 1965:154; Fielding 1953:137; Loch 1968:148-9), British aid worker Barbara Toy was critical of Greek Cypriots' refusal to kill unwanted or stray pets, which she thought merely prolonged suffering (Toy 1970:122). As events in Cyprus spiralled out of control from the 1950s onwards, the increasingly hostile and eventually violent behaviour of locals towards the British seemed inexplicable to most writers of the time. Whilst acknowledged to be lovers of independence, the Greeks were thought to value life and to regret having to kill (Smith, Ashley 1948:95; Travis 1970:132). Evan John was unusual in arguing that there was a divergence in attitudes between mainland Greeks and those of Cyprus. To him, it seemed that the Cypriots "lack all the most typical virtues of the modern Greek, his very great courage, his energy and fair-mindedness" (John 1954:86). Other travel writers struggled to reconcile the actions of Greeks during the Cyprus troubles and

the Civil War with their support for a more noble cause in the earlier
1940s. Toy, who often had to be accompanied on her travels through
Cyprus by an escort from the UN force stationed there, ventured that "fear
must certainly have been the motive that turned the pleasure-loving Greek
Cypriot into a violent killer" (1970:133). Penelope Tremayne, working as
a nurse in Cyprus, accused the press and the communists of driving a
wedge between the British and the Greeks (1958:9, 83). At the same time,
the desire for democracy, under which banner many fought such battles,
was being frequently noted in travel accounts as a Greek characteristic.

In the face of such high profile instability, many travel writers
observed and commented upon the Greek interest in politics. This was a
feature of 50% of 1940s texts, 59% during the following ten years, and
55% in the 1960s, the decade in which the colonels' coup took place.
Overall, the majority (55%) of mid-twentieth century accounts mention
the Greeks conversing about politics, often described as the favourite topic
for men at their café tables. "Armchair politics" was characterized as a
"popular pursuit" (Finer 1964:60), "almost a national pastime" (Patmore
1944:20), or "the Greeks' favourite spectator sport" (Kubly 1970:220).
British travellers frequently found themselves engaged in discussion about
political developments back home, with locals surprisingly well informed
about international current affairs and crises. Some writers argued that
Greek society was notably egalitarian. According to Dilys Powell, there
was "no more democratic society than a Greek country community"
(1941:121), and two decades later Joseph Braddock likewise found "true
democracy in Greece" (1967:24). Such views of Greece as having
"practically no class distinctions" (Patmore 1944:22) may, in part, be
attributed to comparison and frustration with attitudes in Britain at that
time. But the portrayal of the Greeks as interested in political
developments and systems also had much to do with readings of the
ancient world. Some writers made their belief in continuity explicit, as
with Lawrence Durrell's statement that "Greeks have always been the
world's greatest democrats" (1957:135). Ancient precedents might provide
explanations for modern problems. The weakness of classical city-states
unable to work together "remains to this day in modern Greece, in that
they cannot renounce their violent partisanship carried to the point of
disunity" (Bell 1961:97). In discussing pre-First World War Greece,
Compton Mackenzie was led

> to wonder whether there be something in the very air of Hellas which
> forbids prolonged unity. Is the struggle between oligarchy and democracy

with the occasional intervention of tyranny endemic in the birthplace of European politics? (1960:40)

As we saw earlier, due to their defeat of the invading Persians the ancient Greeks were widely regarded as the saviours as well as the originators of the political ideal adopted by modern Western European culture. In the "cradle of democracy" (Smith, M. 1965:85), the heroes of Marathon were "the first but by no means the last of Greeks who have died in defending Europe from the east" (Warner 1950:148). Travel writers such as Eric Forbes-Boyd were thus extremely willing to find that "the birthplace of democracy is still the most democratic of countries" (1964:129). This was, obviously, a particular reading of the Greek past. Only some of the ancient city-states ever practised democracy (thus Athenian history being emphasised over, say, Spartan), and even these did not admit women and slaves to active participation. Travel writers were transferring to the modern inhabitants of Greece the same political interests and beliefs that they ascribed to the ancient people.

Religious beliefs were also a consistent theme for travel writers. In 66% of texts the Greeks were recorded as possessing what Christopher Kininmonth called "sure and unquestioning faith" (Kininmonth 1949:46-7), in Orthodox Christianity or superstition. Easter was the religious observance most often recounted at length by writers, usually with suggestions that piety was shown in the fasting and the outpourings of emotion during the ceremonies (e.g. Bull 1967:4ff; Clift 1958:200ff; Kanelli 1965:50ff). Some treated the differences between Greek Orthodox and Church of England as further proof that a refreshing attitude to life had remained in Greece when it had died in the West. The enthusiastic participation in festivals could be explained as a lack of "the Protestant tendency to separate religion from everyday enjoyment" (Balfour 1951:71). Christopher Kininmonth contrasted the "passionate belief" of the Orthodox Greeks on Syra with the "lifeless" Easter ceremony of the Catholic minority on the island (1949:22). Only 18% of texts contained references to people being anti-religion or non-believing, and no writer made this point regularly (see tables 5 and 7). Occasionally an author suggested that people attending a religious ceremony or exhibiting the outward signs of faith were in reality not particularly strong in their beliefs (e.g. Andrews 1959:169; Carroll 1965:58, 60-1; Travis 1970:198). George Mikes, for example, maintained that "the country is a land of practising Orthodox church-goers without too much ardent religious feeling" (1965:51). But even those Greeks who "profess no interest in the Church" were said to fast nonetheless (Warner 1950:63). C. P. Lee was unusual in stating that the "average" Greek was not "devout" (1957:148).

A number of travel writers suggested that the Christianity currently practised in Greece had its origins in antiquity. Greek religion was "unbroken as the flow of a river through the centuries" (Vvvyan 1955:72). Ancient gods survived in new forms: "Apollo has become St. Elias of the mountain tops; Neptune has become dear, safe St. Nicholas" (Kanelli 1965:90). Practices and traditions also derived from ancient worship. Xan Fielding suggested that "anyone with doubts about the pagan source of peasant Christianity should attend an Orthodox feast" (Fielding 1953:81). The most important celebration for the Virgin was on 15th August, "exactly superceding the ancient pagan festival of the goddess Diana" (Carroll 1965:60). Easter celebrations could be traced to the former "Lesser Eleusinia", which had marked the return of Persephone from the underworld, according to Lawrence Durrell (1953:187). Stanley Evans, despite—or perhaps because of—his position as chancellor of Southwark Cathedral, was emphatic about pagan elements in the Orthodox Church.

> I doubt not, the ancient gods still dwell in the top-most snows [of Mount Olympus]. It was here that they were born and here that they return for refuge. They have been beaten but not destroyed and those who will study the folk-lore of Greece as it is today will find customs enough on particular Christian saints days which, under the guise of honouring St. X, are really intended to safeguard from the fiery darts of the inhabitants of Olympus who excel in the fields of fertility if nowhere else. And in this Greece does not stand alone. There are few countries today which are as securely removed from paganism as we like to think. (Evans 1965:60-1)

Those from the Western Church who found the Orthodox so strange could readily—and often condescendingly—use paganism as an explanation. Those who desired to find the ancient past in the Greece of the present had every interest in showing Greek Orthodox traditions as different from Roman Catholicism and Protestantism.

Writers also emphasised that Greeks believed in the ongoing existence of pagan gods and spirits (as opposed to their transmutation into Christian figures), often thought to be roaming the Greek countryside in search of mischief. Pan, for example, "is still alive on the hills he has always haunted, and . . . in the hearts of his own people" (Wigram 1947:41). There were also said to be vampires, centaurs, nereids, maenads and other malevolent spirits in modern Greece (e.g. Durrell, L. 1945:98-9; Fielding

1953:196-8; Leigh Fermor 1958:195-6, 168-70; Wigram 1947:114, 157-8). It is significant that many of the names used by travel writers for these creatures have their origins in ancient mythology. Joseph Braddock explicitly "delights to find" in local myths "memories of classical antiquity" (1970:146). The intention was to explore modern superstitions by expressing them in terms that were familiar to classically educated readers. Writers explained that the Greeks "still believe in magic and in the power of magic to keep away evil" (Whelpton 1954:122). The most common superstitious practices were people crossing themselves, spitting, or the provision of amulets, all as protection from the evil eye. These too could be regarded as continuities. For example, Barbara Whelpton observed a ferry leaving port.

> Most of the passengers made the sign of the Cross and offered up a prayer for protection on the journey, much, as hundreds of years ago the ancient Greek sailors must have offered up a prayer to Poseidon, god of the sea. (Whelpton 1954:66)

As I noted before, travel writing of this period was joined on bookshelves by the fruits of anthropological research in Greece. Though they were by no means the only anthropologists to consider this area of Greek life, Richard and Eva Blum provided the most extensive treatment of religious beliefs. They recorded village stories about malevolent spirits or demons (1970:12, 13, 95), magic and magicians (14, 17, 22), miracles (45), augury (63), the evil eye (43), the power of saints (88), and nereids (112). John Campbell (1964) also noted superstitions as part of his study of the Sarakatsani, a nomadic shepherding people: old women feared because "knowledge of magic techniques and remedial procedures for the evil eye are attributed to them" (290); newborn children visited by the three fates (329); bands of male and female devils in the countryside (332-3); and bodies returning from the grave "in a hideous distended form often to terrify members of their own family" (337). Juliet du Boulay identified a duality in villagers' religious thinking.

> These beliefs fall roughly into two categories, one derived from Christian Orthodoxy, and the other from the religious beliefs of pagan or "folk" philosophy which persist still into the present day and underlie much of the villagers' religious thought. (du Boulay 1974:51)

Anthropologists of the period had a particular interest in emphasising the primitive nature of Greece. Indeed, the imperative to study "unsophisticated" societies determined the choice of Greece over some other Mediterranean countries, and the focus on the rural over the urban. Most anthropologists represented positively the religious beliefs of their subjects. Du Boulay judged the orthodoxy of her villagers to be "genuine" (1974:52), and whilst Campbell's Sarakatsani "have never been regular churchgoers" they nevertheless "have deep faith" (1964:321-2). Campbell suggested that Greeks found useful role models in Christianity. For men, "Christ is the ideal of continence and selfless sacrifice", whilst the "modesty, virginal attitudes, and selfless love" of Mary was admired in women (Campbell 1964:272). Thus, the family became "an earthly reflection of the Heavenly Family of God the Father, the Mother of God, and Christ" (Campbell 1964:37). Anthropology, then, created a portrait by professional observers of a simple, healthy belief system, untouched by cynicism and linked to the past. This served to legitimize travel writers who looked to antiquity to explain modern Greek attitudes.

Within 66% of travel books, authors found resemblances between Greek individuals or groups they encountered and historical or mythical figures from antiquity. Deities were most frequent: Aphrodite (Braddock 1967:36, 116; Dodge 1955:122), Athena (Kimbrough 1957:192), Apollo (Krippner 1957:109), Zeus (Powell 1973:153; Whelpton 1954:32-3), Hermes (Golding 1955:107; Kubly 1970:83), Adonis (Vyvyan 1955:92), Bacchus (Kininmonth 1949:38), and many others. Piping shepherds were often viewed as Pan, or a faun (e.g. Durrell, L. 1945:116; Toy 1970:86). As a teacher, Lawrence Durrell faced a class where the list of names read "like the *dramatis personae* to a Greek tragedy"; Aphrodite "appropriately enough, was the most spirited and most difficult of the girls" and was "indeed as beautiful as her counterpart in myth was supposed to be" (Durrell, L. 1957:130). Ancient Greek sculpture, for so long regarded as the pinnacle of artistic achievement, sprang to many writers' minds when seeking descriptions for the appearance of those they met on their mid-century travels. Occasionally, the resemblance was to a single work of art. Patrick Anderson encountered a version of the bronze charioteer found at Delphi (1958:132), and Derek Patmore photographed a shepherd who "recalls the famous statue of the Moschophoros", the calf-bearer now in the Acropolis Museum (1944:97). Usually, however, writers contented themselves with a less specific assertion about the look of ancient sculpture. Duncan Forbes, for example, observed Greeks he met on a train.

The sharp noses, bright eyes and half kindly, half cynical smiles reflected with remarkable faithfulness the features that lie in profile on the old vases and stand out full face on the old statues. (1970:44)

Girls filing past Xan Fielding looked "as if a classical frieze had suddenly come to life" (Fielding 1953:230). Greek dancing had "the same steps and movements as in the ancient tomb friezes" (Coles 1965: footnote to 197), or was related to "the Dionysian rites painted on ancient vases" (Kubly 1970:50).

The ancient theatre was recalled in references to staging and authors. Robert Liddell found some "old women [who] till the fields in the timeless dress of their kind, looking like the chorus of an ancient play" (1965:15). Patrick Anderson suggested that in Athens it was not "unusual to find in the people about one a character from Theophrastos or Menander or Aristophanes" (1963:194). Mortal characters for comparison were sometimes taken from classical history, but more often from myth, literature or plays. On Clift's island, respectable locals were giving a foreign lothario a wide berth, just as "the citizens of Thebes locked up their daughters when Dionysus entered their city" (Clift 1959:143). Nick, Robert Liddell's driver, was "one with the machine, a kind of mechanized centaur" (1965:15), and Evan John encountered an old man "like some lovably hideous Socrates" (John 1954:77). Characters from Homer were used numerous times in the travel writing of this period, showing the extent to which authors assumed that readers would be familiar with the stories of the Trojan War and Odysseus: Hector, Achilles (Fielding 1953:80; Liddell 1965:117), Penelope (Pollard 1955:141), the suitors of Penelope, and Nausicaa's maidens (Golding 1955:217, 175).

Few writers frequently made classical comparisons. Some attempted to avoid seeking the past in the present. In tables 5-7, "negative" refers to occasions when writers argued against classical parallels. A boat captain was said not to have the "slightest resemblance to Charon" (Bull 1967:52). The dancing at a festival failed to become the excess of a "bacchanalia" (Smith, Ashley 1948:48). However, as I noted in previous chapters, travellers in Greece were usually more familiar with the ancient than the modern people. C. C. Vyvyan admitted to knowing nothing about modern Greeks: "my familiar Greek friends lived in the pages of Homer and Euripides" (1955:12). As a result, many writers claimed to find it difficult to keep the past at bay. Christopher Kininmonth confessed that "we English particularly can rarely see modern Greece without the ghost of its past intruding" (1949:203). Brenda Chamberlain was plunged into a "suddenly archaic Greece" by an unexpected encounter with goats (1965:78).

The use of classical comparison enabled an author to suggest a link to the past without having to provide an explanation of how and to what extent this may have occurred. At times, however, writers went beyond commenting upon appearance, behaviour or way of life, to suggest actual continuity of population. About one-third of writers explicitly discussed the origins of the people of modern Greece. Some were very clear about the existence of a racial connection with the ancients. Duncan Forbes described the Greeks as the "racial descendants of the victors of Salamis" (1970:44). To C. C. Vyvyan, similarly, the Greeks were the "lineal descendants of Demosthenes" (1955:61). Evan John, however, considered Cypriots as "of dubious racial origin" (John 1954:86). Most writers took a moderate position, neither denying the presence of ancient blood in modern veins, nor claiming the existence of racially pure survivals (see tables 5 and 6). Robert Liddell explicitly stated that the people of the Mani were neither purely of ancient descent, nor wholly of foreign extraction.

> The Maniots are Spartans and Melings [Slavs], and their blood has been further mixed with that of people who have come at many times from many places to take refuge in this remote region. (1958:105)

Arthur Foss emphasised the presence of, for example, "Italian blood", "Norman blood", and a Maltese minority, on various Greek islands (1969:89, 124-5, 187-8, 101). During the Second World War British propaganda countered Hitler's Aryan vision with the proposition that racial strength was not attributable to purity but to the mixing of blood. It was promoted as a virtue that the British were created from the mingling of Celts, Romans, Vikings, Normans, and others. In this climate it seemed natural for post-war travel writers to portray the people of contemporary Greece as forged from ancient Greeks, Turks, Albanians, and so on. Osbert Lancaster explicitly stated that he did not view the Greek "racial hotch-potch" as a negative, but as "testimony to the national vitality" (1947:17, 19).

This reading of racial identity did not necessitate denying that ancient physical or behavioural characteristics had been retained by the modern Greeks. After all, such qualities had been manifest in their heroic stand during the war, when they had emulated their ancestors at Thermopylae. Their actions in 1941 had earned the Greeks "the right to be counted in the line of descent from the greatness of the ancient world" (Powell 1941:179). John Pollard came not to believe "that the old Greek stock has died out altogether", apparently because "the shepherd boy that I met at Sparta would have passed for an ancient Greek anywhere" (1955:197). W.

A. Wigram argued that "the Cretan has kept the build and often the feature of his Minoan forebears" (1947:208). The view of many writers, then, was that it would be foolish to argue that ancients and moderns were unrelated. But how was it that characteristics had been preserved through the centuries? Some offered pseudo-scientific explanations. Wigram (1947:164, 208) suggested that as the races mixed the Greeks biologically came out on top, whereas Colin Simpson argued that there was "minimal intermixture of the two races" during the Turkish occupation (1969:46). More general, however, was the view that culture rather than genetics was of primary importance. Leslie Finer believed that "there has never been such a thing as a pure Greek race", even in ancient times, but he postulated that the people "assimilate without becoming assimilated", still "preserving their own identity" throughout the Ottoman period (Finer 1964:11, 14). Patrick Balfour maintained that "since the days of Byzantium the Cypriots have been Greek by language, religion and culture", and "beneath their acceptance of foreign domination, a certain obstinate sense of Greekness survived" (1951:207-8). In his foreword to Blum and Blum (1970), Prince Peter of Greece reiterated the official line that racial background was

> immaterial when considering Hellenism, an all-embracing outlook on life which has shown itself capable, as other superior cultures have also, of assimilating strangers and foreigners, even enemies, whatever their racial origin.

He stated that "modern Greeks are the cultural continuators if not the physical heirs of the original Hellenes" (Blum and Blum 1970:ix).

These ideas were also promoted via the work of contemporary professional anthropologists. John Davis was later to condemn his colleagues' "assumptions of continuity—historical and geographical—which are not spelled out, and which should be argued, if an impression of potpourri is to be avoided" (1977:253). Davis is referring to work such as that by Campbell who, when discussing the importance of prestige for Greeks, inserted as a footnote his view that "in some respects there are obvious parallels with Homeric society" (1964:263). After accompanying his wife—Ernestine Friedl—on her fieldwork, H. L. Levy published an article concerning the division of property amongst brothers by casting lots. Levy described this practice as a "persistence", a "cultural trait [which] has survived, passed down from generation to generation, through the centuries of Roman, and later of Turkish domination" (Levy 1956:44). However, this was not a "fossilized relic", since it had been "*elaborated* by our villagers, or their forebears more or less remote" (Levy 1956:44, my emphasis). Thus, Levy recognized that the modern practice varied from the ancient, but he nevertheless chose to view it as essentially continuous. As I suggested in chapter two, by the mid-twentieth century Greece had long been promoting its nation status, both to foreigners and its own people, by emphasising the continuity from antiquity of material culture and population. Friedl therefore had some justification when she argued that it was not merely observers but

> the people of Vasilika [who] think of themselves as Greeks with a set of ethnic characteristics which they believe they have shared with the inhabitants of the country in historical continuity from classical Greek times, through Byzantium, into the present. (1962:106).

According to Friedl (1962:106), these inherited qualities included: "the desire for political independence and the willingness to fight for it against overwhelming odds"; "the love of talk and of political conversation in particular"; "love of freedom"; and hospitality.

Travel writer Carola Matthews explained that she found Greek origins complicated.

> Were the ethnologist to take over at this point, his [sic] list of Greek complexions would be infinite, for history has supported geography in producing one of the most complex races inside Europe. (1968:1-2)

For anthropologists, as for travel writers, the classical world provided a ready storehouse of references which could be used to render familiar the traditions and people of mid-twentieth century Greece. Often this was an intellectual sleight of hand, with the conjuring up of an ancient person, belief or practice implying—without further explanation—that there was some real connection rather than being mere coincidence. From the reaction of a later travel writer, Neil Macvicar, to seeing a word familiar to him from ancient Greek (*stasis*) employed to denote a bus stop, we might derive the term "telescoping": "during that blink of time two millennia had been telescoped" (Macvicar 1990:24). The endpaper illustration for Emily Kimbrough's *Forever Old, Forever New* (1965) exemplifies this process. An imaginary temple pediment contains a double row of sculptural figures in parallel poses. The upper set includes a reclining warrior, chariot, and griffin. These are replaced in the lower row by sunbathers, cars, and a poodle. When observing modern Greeks, the ancient world was never far from the travel writer's—or reader's—mind.

(ii) The Greeks as Pastoral and Timeless

In the wake of the conflicts of the 1940s the capital of Greece underwent a transformation. The population of "Greater Athens" (including Piraeus) has been calculated at 1,378,586 in 1951, rising a decade later to 1,852,709, and to 2,540,242 by 1971 (Vermeulen 1983:115). Few observers were complimentary about the aesthetic effects of this growth upon the city. Alexander Eliot warned readers of the 1960s that "the capital is modern and faceless" with "mile upon mile of concrete office and apartment warrens" (1964:13). Urban sprawl and pollution, globalisation and homogeneity, were not what most Westerners expected or wanted of Greece. Instead, travellers of the mid-century period showed a determination to focus on Greece as a primitive and backward-looking country.

Anthropologists had professional reasons for portraying the country as undeveloped and largely untouched by modernity. Although within the discipline there was a new "intellectual curiosity to discover how an anthropologist might approach the study of European society" (Campbell 1992:149), this was still a time "when teaching was based on 'exotic' classics" (Kenna 1992:160). Many of the pioneers of modern Mediterranean studies felt that their colleagues working in far-flung areas did not see the same value in working geographically—or culturally— closer to home. Decades later Margaret Kenna recalled:

> However long the catalogue of my physical miseries, it could never validly compare, I felt, with the dangers experienced by fieldworkers in Africa, South America, New Guinea, on whose texts I had been brought up as an undergraduate. I was conscious that being a Mediterraneanist was thought rather odd and not "real fieldwork" by others, including my fellow students, some of whom carried out fieldwork in Africa. (Kenna 1992:155)

Anthropologists in Greece and other Mediterranean countries therefore sought ways to demonstrate that their work was equal to that undertaken in more distant parts of the world. In order to show that the way of life they studied was as "primitive as [that of] every other colleague", Mediterranean anthropologists chose "to work in the marginal areas of the region—in the mountains, in the small peasant communities" (Davis 1977:7). Greece emerged in anthropology as "isolated from external influences . . . [with] no cities, little immigration, little trade" (Davis 1977:20). In introducing her own village study, Friedl conceded that

the majority of those interested in learning the ways of life of the co-heirs
of their own civilisation have concentrated on what have been called "folk"
or "peasant" societies, or, to phrase it more descriptively, the rural
population of modern nations. (1962:2)

Some anthropologists were aware that life in Greece showed signs of
development. Juliet du Boulay set out to highlight change: "this book is a
study of a phenomenon which is becoming all too frequent in the present
day—a dying village community" (1974:3).

Instead of extreme physical hardship and a high degree of self-sufficiency,
people began to reduce their hours of toil in the fields, to live more
comfortably in their homes, and to develop a way of life involving
increasing dependence on more modernized communities and a gradual
acquaintance with urban ways of life. (1974:247)

Du Boulay seized the opportunity to criticize change modelled on the
West.

Whatever the fate of this society, and whatever may have been its
limitations and its defects, there is no doubt that when it was integrated to a
living tradition it gave life both dignity and meaning—qualities which are
conspicuously lacking in the type of society that threatens to succeed it.
(1974:258)

Most, however, represented the life of the settlement they studied as
primitive, slow and unchanging. Campbell's community of "Greek-
speaking transhumant shepherds known as Sarakatsani" lived in simple
huts made largely of wood, mud, dung, and reeds or grasses (1964:1, 33).
The inhabitants of Friedl's village were "farmers and shepherds" using
primitive equipment: "the pack saddle of wood and leather is of a design
that has remained virtually unchanged since Homeric times" (1962:8, 30).
As a result, "the pace of movement is always slow even when it is most
purposeful . . . The pace seems to be set by the slow walk of a loaded
horse or mule or donkey" (Friedl 1962:16). This was an archaic, frozen
society. As anthropologist Michael Herzfeld later commented, Greece was
made to conform to a "vestigially survivalist thesis—that is, an argument
that treats the values of local societies as relatively simple features
surviving from a prestatist era" (Herzfeld 1987:8). The "modern" Greeks
became the exotic "other" within Europe.

Whilst the professional imperative to locate primitiveness was not so
strong for travel writers, Greece was nevertheless preferred by travellers

and readers as a country of the past in the present. In 86% of mid-century texts, writers noted the simplicity of such features as housing and sanitation, and the mode of making a living as being pastoral or agricultural. This was made a consistent theme in almost half of the texts of the period by the inclusion of five or more references (table 7). In compiling such figures, I did not note every mention of an olive tree, but only instances where writers referred to fishing, shepherding, or engagement in one of a range of other agricultural activities. However extensive the movements of the travel writer—whether they were all but stationary as a resident of a particular community, or spending just two weeks travelling to see a range of ancient monuments—Greece was viewed as a series of backward, invariably village, communities. For Michael Osler, when viewed from home Greece was "a place where Americans and classical enthusiasts visit graceful ruins." Once travelling there however, "it is the villages that grow into one's awareness as the cities recede" (Osler 1957:102).

This was "a world of donkeys, cobbled streets, bare rock, bare-handed toil, simple to primitive everywhere" (Knowles 1964:199). This "civilization at the bottom of the economic ladder" (Knowles 1964:199) could certainly leave some of the inhabitants in difficulties. As Michael Osler noted, "wars of one sort or another have reduced the country to a poverty that is almost destitution" (1957:117). But "simplicity of life" apparently resulted from choice as much as necessity since "most village Greeks retain a Doric love for a simple diet" (Kanelli 1965:42). As a country where "every man and woman has roots in the land" (Powell 1941:101), urban life was abnormal. But travellers from abroad might have to spend several days in the city of Athens if they wished to view the ancient monuments in detail. The modern city received some coverage in travel writing, often focusing upon its poor modern architecture, pollution, noise and traffic, or picturesque areas like the Plaka (Wills 2006). But writers rarely commented on the style of life in the capital. Some succeeded in infiltrating the Athenian social scene, receiving invitations to dinner parties and embassies (such examples of "sophisticated" living are recorded within the "negative" figures in tables 5-7). Dilys Powell attempted to collapse cultural difference by pointing out that Athens had its "fashionable society, just as any European capital" (1941:81). Stays in and descriptions of other cities such as Salonica—whose antiquities were regarded as much less interesting—were invariably brief. A very few writers noted the presence of factories and their workers (e.g. Kimbrough 1957:100-1; Toy 1970:15, 47). But Patrick Balfour suggested that the countryside was the Greeks' true home: "even the industrial worker remains at heart, a peasant, ready to return there [to the land] if he loses his job" (1951:199). In Crete, Robert Payne expressed great delight in travelling away from built-up Herakleion to "villages where the men were apple-cheeked and still wore the ancient Cretan costume" (1965:31).

This depiction of the "primitive simplicity of the lives of these country people" (Mais and Mais 1962:140) was rarely intended to be derogatory. Monica Krippner was unusual in damning the lack of spirit and development.

> In the countryside and provincial towns there is an air of lethargy and hopelessness, the people are shackled by old customs, conditions are often extremely primitive, and all the innate energy and vitality is sapped from the peasants as they grimly eke a living out of a barren unproductive soil. (1957:28)

For most writers however, the Greeks retained a "natural sense of dignity" (Finer 1964:47) in the face of such adversity. Lawrence Durrell romanticized the Greek condition as "the naked poverty that brings joy without humiliation" (1953:76). The existence of "progress" was sometimes difficult for writers to ignore, but—outside of Athens—this was usually felt to have been assimilated sympathetically into the Greek landscape and lifestyle. Leslie Finer thought that the Greeks had thus far preserved the "immediacy of man's contact with his physical environment and with his fellows" (1964:82). Visitors "will find that the modern Greeks have kept their knowledge of the magic simpleness of things" (Braddock 1967:13).

Travel writers, including Joseph Braddock, found a sense of "timelessness".

> One may escape for a while from the tensions and triviality of a too competitive industrial society of wage-slaves, avoid the daily routine of the human beehive, and step straight into an ageless pastoral, where the wind of poetry has never ceased blowing. (Braddock 1967:14)

Monica Krippner agreed that "life has a continuity in these [Aegean] islands and the routine has changed little in centuries" (1957:159). This was a country where time had—and continued to—pass more slowly. According to Eric Forbes-Boyd, in Nauplia "life moves in slow motion"

(1964:69). Likewise, after landing in Corfu for his first visit in twenty-one years, Gerald Durrell quickly found himself

> enveloped in that curious sense of timelessness that is one of the island's chief charms. Soaked in sunshine and food we soon attained the Nirvana where you know that each year has four million days, and each will be as perfect as this one. (Forte 1964:58)

For the Greeks too, "time does not exist" (Vyvyan 1955:115). A great many writers commented on the necessity of adjusting to "Greek time" with regard to appointments, travel timetables, building work, opening hours, and bureaucracy. For example, according to Robert Payne "ships leave when they want to leave" (1965:9). This often proved frustrating. Gillian Mais contented herself with the cool observation that "the Greek sense of time is very different from ours" (Mais and Mais 1962:149). Michael Carroll, however, commended this "country where the national philosophy wisely maintains that a few hours here or there will make little difference to anyone" (1965:33). In the 1960s historian E. P. Thompson was arguing that the shift towards "clock time" in Britain had been a defining feature of the move towards a modern, industrialized society (Urry 1995:4-5, 19-20). The lack of awareness of "clock time" among the Greeks could therefore be seen by travel writers as a relic of an earlier age. Emily Kimbrough explicitly maintained that the Greek sense of time (or, rather, lack of it) represented continuity from ancient times (1965:125).

The sociologist Dean MacCannell has discussed how "in modernity the nonmodern must be construed as pre-, as historically past to modernity's present" (as summarized in Kaplan, C. 1996:59). As apparently unaware of time and unchanging in their lifestyle, the Greeks were seen to be exempt from the normal passage of time—they were atemporal. By representing them thus, it became easier for travel writers to maintain that they were looking at an ancient people in the present. Xan Fielding saw the Cretans stretching back to the time of Homer: "by-passed by history, its inhabitants are outstanding in the evidence which their customs and traditions afford of the survival of an unspoilt people of the Heroic Age" (Fielding 1953:302). Alternatively, customs might "derive direct from the classical age", including "costume, domestic habits, cuisine" (Coles 1965:52-3). As in the 1800s, Greeks were evidently "expected to play the part of the revenant, primordial ancestor of Europe itself" (Herzfeld 1987:25). In the mid-twentieth century, primitiveness usually formed part of a positive representation, linked to writers' desires and expectations of what they thought of as "Greek". Nevertheless, there was an element of condescension in this approach. In a 1991 study, John Barrell showed that nineteenth century British writers in Egypt represented local people as "close to the earth" in their lifestyle. This served to separate Egyptian from Westerner, because it was believed that civilized people had managed to place distance between themselves and their Biblical origins in "dust" (1991:106-7). In Greece, people had remained undeveloped, unlike their guests.

(iii) The Greeks as "Oriental"

George Mikes argued that the Greeks often looked down on tourists—for their clothes, attitude to money, and ignorance—but did not take advantage of them (1965:7ff). However, in 37% of texts it was suggested that some form of financial or sexual exploitation of foreigners had been attempted. This ranged from overcharging and harassment by street vendors, to Greek men who viewed young female tourists as easy sexual prey. John Pollard was unusual in listing a number of unfortunate experiences: "ceaseless assaults" from beggars, overpriced hotel rooms, and a guide who stole his camera (1955:13-4, 28, 109, 200). In Athens, Herbert Kubly found that even the policemen participated in scams to entice tourists into bars serving overpriced drinks (1970:177-83). Ashley Smith bought a fake gold ring, having been deceived through the "superior intelligence and psychological insight of the Greeks" (1948:53). In relating such behaviour, several writers offered mitigating factors. It seemed understandable that, faced with Western wealth and the predilection of the young to wear very little on holiday, some Greeks should seek to take what is apparently being offered. After all, to a Greek who might never even have been as far as Athens, it was logical to suppose that any traveller from Britain must be extremely rich. John Pollard discovered this attitude when the money he proffered for an overnight stay was dismissed as being insufficient (1955:154). Phoebe-Lou Adams implied that it was the fault of tourists to Rhodes for being so gullible: she found "any number of antique shops where the unwary can acquire, at considerable expense, articles that the Rhodians sensibly wish to get rid of" (1965:30).

It also seemed understandable to most writers that, for a member of a society where women were expected to stay remote from men before marriage, a foreign woman who exhibited herself must be seeking a sexual relationship. The place of women within the Greek household and community was often described in negative terms, as a remnant of a less enlightened society. There were clearly defined gender roles, "older than recorded history", in which women carried out the domestic chores and gave up their seats on buses to men (Clift 1958:52ff). Writers considered emancipation a proper aspiration, and female travellers who became resident in Greece found it difficult to come to terms with the expectations placed upon them. Sheelagh Kanelli was, since her marriage to a Greek, in a good position to observe that a woman "leads a life of subjection to the male" (1965:93). However, examples of Greeks trying to take sexual advantage of female travellers were recorded quite rarely. Often such incidents were attributed to the behaviour and dress of the visitors. Ian Brook criticized female tourists on Rhodes for offering a "come-on incitement to molestation" (Brook 1971:43-4). Carola Matthews outlined the process by which Greek men were becoming more flirtatious.

> The foreign girl who thinks that all Greeks are prepared for anything, does not realise that in places untouched by tourists it is unlikely that a man will make a pass at her . . . only in those areas more influenced by Athenians and foreigners the vicious circle expands, and no one knows who was the first seducer. (1968:127)

This portrayal of sexual predation played on Western fears of the immoral Orient as a place of dangerous sex. As Edward Said showed in *Orientalism*, this has in recent times emerged in the film and television characterization of the Arab as "an oversexed degenerate" (Said 1985:287). But, since the nineteenth century, "the East" has been believed to contain not merely predatory men but also the *opportunity* for sex of a "libertine and less guilt-ridden" sort, and many, mostly male, travellers have written of their search for it (Said 1985:190). Greek men were shown by travel writers as reproducing (and appropriating) this orientalist discourse when they claimed to offer better sex to foreign women than could be experienced in the West.

> Strapping young Rhodians strut the beaches convinced that *they* are what the Nordic blondes in bikinis came for, because "Swedish man is not such good lover as Grik". (Simpson 1969:87, original emphasis)

Greece was less often read as a place where local men made themselves available to male sex tourists. In reality, Athens may have provided "a haven for European homosexuals in the interwar period" (Roessel 2003:245), but it did not emerge as such in published novels or travel accounts. Perhaps this was due to readers' perceived sensibilities. David Roessel suggests that "the heterosexual world was not going to embrace a conception of Greece, the birthplace of Western civilization, as the site of transient assignations, often homosexual" (Roessel 2003:248).

Some writers attributed apparently strange or threatening behaviour to cultural misunderstanding. Such incidents are recorded in tables 5-7 as "negative" examples of seeking to take advantage. Carola Matthews initially assumed that intense personal questioning was a form of sexual proposition (1968:158-62; see material on "curiosity" earlier in this chapter). Phoebe-Lou Adams caused uproar when she falsely accused a waiter of short-changing her (1965:15-7). When Penelope Tremayne's life was threatened in Cyprus, she claimed that her would-be attackers "were not monsters", but merely "at the end of their nervous strength" (1958:52-4). Another perceived cultural divide was the level of noise at which life was led, a subject for comment in 78% of texts. According to Herbert Kubly, Athens was the second noisiest place in the world (1970:38). In the craft quarter of Nicosia, Laurie Lee experienced "such a banging and slapping, sawing and hammering, snipping and nailing, singing and shouting, as to make the head reel" (Lee and Keene 1947:23). Vehicles, animals, music, voices—all contributed to the volume of a typical Greek community as portrayed in these accounts. There is condescension in Fielding's characterization of the Cretans as possessing a "childish passion for noise" (1953:28). Ken Duxbury was equally conscious of the distance between himself and the locals when he was assaulted by "the plaintive, *somewhat Arabic*, wail of a popular Greek song [which] reverberated at full blast in the quivering night air" (Duxbury 1973:22, my emphasis). Much of the sound however, was that of talk. Greeks were described as sociable to the point where they "never seem to lack time to stop and talk to one another" (Braddock 1967:138). This characteristic was underlined through mentioning individuals who were unusually silent or monosyllabic. Nancy Spain found a caïque crew "unlike every other Greek I have ever met", in that "they simply didn't want to talk" (1964:204). Robert Payne was fulsome in his praise for a discreet guide: "to anyone who has listened to Greek guides such quietness, reserve and accuracy appear almost miraculous" (1965:86). Some writers asserted that Greeks "hated solitude and silence" because there was no "inner life" in their heads to keep them occupied (Anderson 1963:33; Krippner 1957:128; Liddell 1954:26). This serious criticism no doubt stemmed from disappointment at finding modern Greece apparently bereft of the level of cultural achievement known from antiquity.

Much of the conversation observed by travel writers took place at coffee shops, where Greek men seemed to spend most of the day. Accusations of Greeks failing to work hard usually came from those writers who sought to become resident in Greece, who almost invariably experienced frustrations in the completion of their housing projects. Purchase, planning permission, building work, and maintenance, were all subject to delays (Wills 2005a). Charmian Clift and her family resided in an inadequate, primitive, ill-equipped house, which their landlady refused to improve (1958:38). Non-resident writers were usually more charitable. In Rhodes, Phoebe-Lou Adams felt that the "lack of opportunity, not laziness, explains the idling youths" (1965:29). Reinhold Schiffer has recently shown how 1930s travellers to the Middle East, like their nineteenth century counterparts, contrasted the "Protestant work ethic, i.e. to work strenuously for their earthly bliss (and, hopefully and indirectly, for their heavenly bliss)", with the Muslim fatalistic outlook which Westerners saw as leading to apathy (Schiffer 2001:313-6). Travel writers in Greece failed to sever their representation of the people from this "lazy oriental" discourse. The Greeks thus became a people of indeterminate status.

Though Robert Bell chose to characterize "busty" women he encountered as having "classical figures" (1961:196), for him Greece represented the "half-way house between Europe and the Middle East" (Bell 1961:25). Most travellers were less phlegmatic, expressing shock when they were confronted by behaviour or traditions they regarded as oriental. "In my ignorance I had dreamed of a classical Greece, but in fact, this is already the East, another world than that of Western Europe." (Chamberlain 1965:24) Observing the "Turkish tradition" of village men smoking long clay pipes, Emily Kimbrough admitted that

> Belatedly we were astonished. Acknowledging a witless unobservance, we excused it by our concentration on the evidences remaining of Ancient Greece. (Kimbrough 1965:122)

In the main however, travel writers were anxious to play down the Eastern connection. Dilys Powell for example, dismissed the idea that it was the "oriental position of women in Greece" which barred them from cafés, by pointing out that "an English country pub is rarely crowded by the wives and daughters of the local farmers and labourers" (Powell 1941:108). This reflected the agenda of the 1940s, establishing Greece as European in order to aid British readers' identification with the Greek people. For this to take place, the legacy of Turkish occupation had, as with physical structures, to be ignored, downgraded or stripped away.

The "disappearance" of the Turkish period allowed the Greeks to become "fixed in time before modern history" (Herzfeld 1987:54). The Greeks were living monuments, alongside the stone ones, to the achievements of antiquity. They provided evidence for the lifestyles and beliefs of the Greek "golden age" over two thousand years before. Mid-twentieth century travellers were, like their counterparts of the 1800s, able to "experience in the present the grandeur of an imagined past" (Galani-Moutafi 2000:208). This required that the Greeks became a people who were largely unaffected by the forces of development and change. The traveller

> recognized a (Greek) present only in those cases where he/she did not see threads of continuity in the relationship between ancient and modern Greece; that present, he/she incorporated it in the category of "foreign" (as unpredictable, odd and undesirable). (Galani-Moutafi 2000:209)

The Turkish past might be recognized where it proved useful as the alleged origin for unpleasant or strange aspects of the Greek character: corruption, dishonesty, sexual predation, laziness, and lack of timekeeping. As Michael Herzfeld explains, Turks have often been portrayed as the antithesis of Europe because of their possession of negative qualities.

> Shiftiness, double-dealing, illiteracy, influence-peddling and rule-bending, disrespect for norms and admiration for cunning individuals who could twist them for their own disadvantage. (Herzfeld 1987:29)

For example, in the nineteenth century both shepherds and officials were able to attribute the practice of animal theft in Crete to "a remnant of the response to Turkish oppression" (Herzfeld 1987:45). It was the occupiers who "had corrupted the Greeks by forcing them to fight Turkish guile with Turkish guile" (Herzfeld 1987:125). Penny Travlou has likewise noted that in guidebooks to Athens it is only the unpleasant aspects of the Greek character—ugliness or poor service—that are attributed to oriental influence (Travlou 2002:112). This allowed Westerners to envisage the Greeks as on a journey, travelling from the darkness of oriental influence into the light of European civilization. The West continued to assist the Greeks in rediscovering and developing their true nature, to strip away the unfortunate accretions of recent centuries. In *The Glory that is Greece*,

Professor Sir John Myres stated that from independence in 1821, the Greek people and nation "grew up out of a fractious childhood" (Hughes, H. 1944:24). The child metaphor was indeed useful to the Western European powers. Across the Middle East in the nineteenth century, the slow pace of life and apparent lack of progress had served to justify European imperial expansion. As an infant nation, Greece would require nurturing, guidance, and possibly discipline, from overseas. Even in the 1940s, a British administrator of Cyprus, Sir Andrew Wright, was said by one contemporary American commentator to have "looked upon the Cypriots as children who needed a firm hand . . . and an occasional spanking" (Holland and Markides 2006:222). The development of the higher cultural achievements which had flowered in ancient Greece—art, literature, theatre, and so on—had been halted by the Turkish occupation and thought by twentieth century Western observers *not* to be flourishing in the present country. Ashley Smith, for example, commented that the artistic products of present-day Greece "look as if six-year-old children could turn them out. Homer drawn in chalks on a plate" (1948:51). The *potential* for creativity might still be there—as travel writers commented when they observed Greeks dancing, for example—but not the sophistication. Cretan villagers seemed to Henry Miller like "uncouth savages" compared with the Minoans (Miller, H. 1942:123). There were two sets of Greeks. Those dwelling in the modern country had retained the "folklore" learning, beliefs, and physical characteristics of the ancients. But others, who had inherited the "higher" learning and culture, had moved West. In the interim between the ancient world and the present, the British had become the conservators of classical culture and values. The late nineteenth century mission in Cyprus, for example, was portrayed as "less to civilize than to *restore*" through contact between "'the height of our present [British] civilisation' and its living ancestors" (Herzfeld 1987:74). Then, as in the mid-twentieth century, the British were Greeks too.

British writers emphasised both their indebtedness and superiority to the Greeks. By endowing the people with many of the same attributes as their ancestors, the traveller was able to find ancient Greece in the modern world. For a classicist, the Greeks were exciting and valuable as "a living supplement to his [*sic*] knowledge and understanding of ancient literature and society" (Friedl 1970:195-6). But, as travellers, British people often felt themselves to be financially and culturally on a higher level to their hosts.[10] In her analysis of the representation of the Greek people in guidebooks to Athens, Penny Travlou found that

where they are connected to the tourist services, hierarchy and authority is
built between the tourist playing the role of the civilised Westerner and the
Athenian as the provider of low quality services but of a generous
personality. (Travlou 2002:120)

But, as I have suggested, travellers could also view their own life and
values as *over*-sophisticated, and idealize the Greeks' simplicity. Robert
Liddell described how "to the sentimental Philhellene it is all just
wonderful; he throws off all his western inhibitions and introversion"
(1958:23-4). For many travellers writing at that time, Greece offered
escape from modern life: "it is the turn of the Greek isles in the constant
search for the remote, the off-beat, the primitive life" (Forbes 1970:126).
Brenda Chamberlain was fleeing a world of "almost-living", in which
people "act under compulsion, at the dictates of a machine-driven
existence" (1965:22). Such travellers hoped to find "a source, or a wonder,
or a sign, to be reassured in our humanity" (Clift 1958:19). In Greece,
primitiveness was a sign of purity, vitality and strength. This had been a
theme as far back as the nineteenth century, when travellers felt they were
setting out from their own countries which were being "transformed far
more rapidly and radically than the nations of the south" (Jenkyns
1980:44). As Mark Mazower has shown, "the idea of modernity in
nineteenth-century Europe, with its sharp sense of time moving ahead fast,
encouraged a view of the Balkans as a place where 'time has stood still'"
(Mazower 2000:27). However, the apparent ahistoricity of a people can
form part of either a positive or negative portrayal. For example, as
Katherine Turner has shown, in their eighteenth century travel writings
both Lady Mary Wortley Montagu and Lady Elizabeth Craven represented
the Turks as ahistorical, but with very different results.

> Montagu combines a respect to Turkish cultural history with a poetic
> imagining of Turkish culture as existing *outside* history and indeed
> politics; Craven constructs an alternative history, within which Turkish
> culture is erased, and the Turks are instead configured as almost pre-
> historic in their barbaric indolence. (Turner, K. 1999:128)

As I have explained, for mid-twentieth century travel writers the concept
of timelessness in Greece usually had positive connotations, except where
influence from Turkey or the West led to practices which inconvenienced
the traveller. Timelessness enabled analogies with ancient events, types
and personalities, which aided the traveller's sense of transportation.

> The portrayal of modern Athenians as reproductions of ancient Greek
> figures is related to the need of tourists to verify on every occasion the

material existence of the "dream land" they are visiting. The ancient Athens: the cradle of Western Civilisation, still existing because her citizens are recognisable on the faces of the inhabitants of the present day. (Travlou 2002:121)

John Knox Forte emphasised that

as one grew to know the people, one realized that one had not *escaped* from civilization, but that one had at last *found* it. After all, it was in Greece that civilization began. (Forte 1964:5, original emphasis)

Travel writers found the ancient Greeks only *partially* preserved—and that is, in truth, the way they wanted it. Greeks could then be kept at a distance, conforming fully to no single identity—Eastern or Western, ancient or modern, primitive or civilized. The representation of the Greeks was formed out of a tension between all of these elements.

CHAPTER FIVE

THE TRANSFORMATION OF GREECE, THE EVOLUTION OF TRAVEL WRITING (1975-2007)

The period from the mid-1970s until the present has seen many of the themes familiar from earlier periods persisting in travel writing. In this chapter, which I do not claim to be exhaustive, I consider the extent to which representations of Greece have evolved in response to the aspirations of travellers, the nature of the publishing trade, and the transformation of the country itself.

The 1970s and '80s witnessed the production of a steady stream of books by what I have termed "stationary travellers", those who stayed in Greece for rather longer than merely a few weeks of holiday. Gerald Durrell followed up the success of *My Family and Other Animals* with two further volumes, *Birds, Beasts, and Relatives* (1969) and *The Garden of the Gods* (1978; the three were later published together as Durrell, G. 2006). Durrell was, of course, writing of his experiences of Corfu in an earlier era, and his characterization of the islanders likewise reflects the past rather than the modern. He describes one family, for example, as "quite well off by peasant standards" (1978:21). In *Fair Prospects* (1976), Glyn Hughes reproduced the familiar concept of the interminable bureaucracy faced by potential residents, in his case the paperwork required for his marriage to an Athenian (Hughes, G. 1976:51). But he also provided a window on momentous events through his testimony about the effects of the colonels' regime upon the country. More typical of this sub-genre of travel book is Austen Kark's *Attic in Greece* (1994). Set in the 1980s, this is described on the cover as "one man's love affair with a country and the comedy of errors and delights which allowed him to live there." In this, Kark's account resembles the domesticity tales of the 1950s and '60s, such as those by Peter Bull, Brenda Chamberlain, and Charmian Clift. Kark also pointed the way to the future, because since the mid-1990s there has been a huge increase in the number of such publications. This has no doubt been assisted by the popularity of books about settling in countries other than Greece. As Sue Arnold commented in a recent review praising Lawrence Durrell's *Bitter Lemons of Cyprus*, "following Peter Mayle's *A Year in Provence*, every expat with a cowshed in Croatia reckons that his [*sic*] hilarious DIY exploits will be a bestseller" (Arnold 2006). Indeed, whilst established publishing houses such as Granta (Storace 1997; Zinovieff 2004), Penguin (MacLean 2004), Duckworth (Shields 2005) and John Murray (Chatto 2005) have been responsible for the dissemination of such work, many titles have in recent years come from smaller companies, including the essentially self published. These have included Yiannis Books of Twickenham (Waller 2004 and 2005; Hounsell 2007), Racing House Press of London (Jinkinson 2005), and Universal Publishers of Florida (Cox 2001).

As we have seen, these authors were joining a long tradition of relocation to Greece, and of writing about the experience. But the demand for migration from Britain seems to have increased greatly over the last decade or so. By the 1990s British tourists were more confident about striking out on their own when they went abroad: many more than in previous decades were booking self-catering apartments rather than all-inclusive hotels (Bray and Raitz 2001:201). Long term residence has seemed the natural extension of a foreign holiday, an aspiration promoted by British television programmes such as *A Place in the Sun*. Sylvia and Terry Cook—editors of a series of volumes called *The Greek-o-File*—have recently claimed that

> Greece is becoming more and more popular as a retirement destination and as a second home for those still working in the UK or trying to divide their time between two life styles. (Cook and Cook 2003:16)

One recent property guide has estimated that half of the buyers on Hydra are foreign (Cambridge 2006:114). In Crete, Anthony Cox discovered that he and his wife had

> deluded ourselves in assuming that there were few foreigners living in these parts . . . Ian, who I met at a Greek language school in Hania, told me that he'd come across a Glaswegian couple, an American bricklayer, a German psychiatrist, an Italian doctor and an Englishman in a remote village who worked for Sotheby's. (Cox 2001:151)

The attractions of life in Greece have been characterized much as they were in the travel writing of earlier decades: "a desire for a better climate, a cheaper life, or even to escape the memories of humdrum life or exhausting life" (Cook and Cook 2003:16). When described in such terms, Greece becomes largely interchangeable with other hot spots in the Mediterranean. Indeed, in an interview for *Greece* magazine, Rosslyn and Derek Atkins claimed to have fallen in love with Crete "because it reminds us of Spain thirty years ago" (*Greece* 2004:38). In contrast, some residents have sought to demonstrate their appreciation that Greece is *not* another Spain. The first volume of *The Greek-o-File* was introduced by its editors thus:

> not for those who revel in the noisy touristy places that could be anywhere in the world, nor for those who expect to find everything English with sunshine when they go abroad, but it is for those who have been captivated by the differences of Greece—the friendly welcome of the locals, the quiet unspoilt villages and resorts, the beauty of coast and countryside and the rich past which seems evident all around. (Cook and Cook 2002:5)

In earlier decades, British residents claimed for themselves a special status, superior to both the native Greeks and to itinerant tourists. But now, with British people having migrated to Greece over several generations, some writers also perceive a separation between themselves and other actual or potential residents. Greece has become a place of residency for the more discerning traveller, "a *quality* country" according to one 2006 property guide (Cambridge 2006:3, my emphasis).[11] Introducing an account in which the writer becomes "part of the village", John Waller comments that "this is a story that too few of the new migrants to the Mediterranean can tell" (Hounsell 2007:8).

After a recent survey of over a thousand people, sociologist Philip L. Pearce has concluded that the most common motives for travel are novelty, to escape or relax, and to strengthen personal relationships (Pearce 2005:58, 66). Pearce found that "personal development motives are emphasised more by people with less travel experience, whereas host-site involvement motives become more evident as their travel experience develops" (Pearce 2005:67). It is therefore not surprising to find that interaction with locals is regarded as important by those whose experience of Greece as tourists has led them to decide to stay in the country. They have wanted to put down roots by establishing meaningful relationships not merely with others from their own countries (e.g. their own families) but with local people. Recent travel writers have positioned themselves as locals by recognizing that at least some changes were overdue in Greece. Katherine Kizilos, for example, accepted that "living in a museum of old

Greek values had only a limited appeal for the people who were stuck in it" (1997:215). Yet, as in earlier decades, whilst Britons of the 1990s onwards claimed to have moved abroad to start a new life, many apparently wanted the Greek lifestyle only on their own terms. When Neil Macvicar expressed his belief that it was desirable for some aspects of Greece to change, he gave examples which conformed to his own comfortable (Western European) existence—piped water, electricity, and telephones (1990:135).

Well worn representations of the Greek people have lingered in travel accounts. The allegedly inefficient and even corrupt nature of Greek services and officials has received much attention. When Austen Kark tried to bring his car into Greece, he was left "fuming about the absurdity of the regulations" (1994:265). He was also told that getting a telephone installed in his house might take five to ten years due to the backlog of requests (Kark 1994:105). Sofka Zinovieff described how personal connections and sometimes bribery would speed up the progress of citizenship applications (2004:43-4, 73-4). She professed to become "annoyed when Greece lives up to its stereotype as an unreliable, dishonest place" (Zinovieff 2004:157). Yet Zinovieff, like so many other writers, looked to the East when forming explanations for unfortunate traits. In her view, the system of officials doing favours in return for gifts was "an old Muslim institution", existing alongside other Turkish survivals such as food and language (Zinovieff 2004:161, 224ff).

Many of the harshest critics of Greece have been those of Greek descent. An early example of an American Greek's odyssey to his homeland was Nicholas Gage's *Eleni* (1983), in which the author sought to confront those involved in the death of his mother during the Civil War. In recent years, however, many more offspring of the Greek diaspora have tried to make sense of their identity through writing. These have included Katherine Kizilos' *The Olive Grove* (1997), George Sarrinikolaou's *Facing Athens* (2004), and Eleni (daughter of Nicholas) Gage's *North of Ithaka* (2004). The younger Gage railed against Greek civil servants.

> They're exhausted by the endless toil of creating hoops for the fearful public to jump through in order to achieve their unrealistic goals of building a house, obtaining a visa or mailing a package. (Gage, E. 2004:58)

Sarrinikolaou, a New Yorker from the age of ten who returned to Athens "to reclaim a space for myself in the city where I was born", described at length the corruption in the public health system: "the extent and quality of care depend on an institutionalized practice of bribery" (2004:ix, 112).

However, whilst such criticisms have continued in travel writing, positive characterizations of Greece have emerged from some unexpected quarters. In the run up to the Olympic Games of 2004, familiar negative representations of Athens were rehearsed in British newspapers as well as in guidebooks and travel writing. In *The Independent*, for example, Guy Alexander wrote that "Athens' Olympic preparations have been laughingly billed as the modern Greek ruins" (Alexander, Guy. 2004:3). Australian travel writer Ann Rickard tried to give a balanced view based on her 2003 visit: "next year, when the Olympics are about to be staged, we are sure Athens will be a place of grandness again, but now it is just an awful mess" (2004:25). After the success of the games and its infrastructure, the media were more generous. During the BBC's live television broadcast of the 2006 Eurovision Song Contest (20th May 2006), veteran commentator Sir Terry Wogan took the opportunity to praise the hosts: "Athens and Greece has been transformed by the success of the Olympic Games." As a result of the Olympic building work, the myth of Greek laziness—an alleged Turkish legacy inspired by orientalism—is finally being challenged. John F. L. Ross argues that "there is no apparent Greek equivalent of Spain's storied *mañana* ('tomorrow') mentality." Instead, Athens is "a bee-hive of frenetic activity, restless change and constant experimentation. A lazy place? Don't believe a word of it" (Ross 1999:18).

Over the past few years travel writing about Greece has not been immune from the phenomenon we might call the "novelty" journey. The antecedents for this were Tim Severin's *The Jason Voyage* (1985), and, likewise reproducing a classical myth, Goran Schildt's earlier *In the Wake of Odysseus* (1953). A couple of recent examples have involved two wheeled travel: *Greece on My Wheels* (2003), with Edward Enfield cycling in the footsteps of Byron, and *Cleopatra's Needle* (2003), in which Anne Mustoe took in Greece en route from London to Cairo, again by bicycle. Rory MacLean's *Falling for Icarus* (2004) concerns an attempt to take to the skies above Crete in a home-made aeroplane. In common with writing on other countries, there has been a sharp division of travel writing from more serious informational sources. Most writing no longer provides the reader with extended historical background on Greece. Peter Greenhalgh and Edward Eliopoulos' 1985 study of their journey *Deep into Mani* belongs to an earlier style of narrative in which observation and history were intertwined. More recently, following in the footsteps of Robert Byron, Christopher Merrill (2004) and Matthew Spencer (2000) have produced thought-provoking accounts of pilgrimages to the monasteries of Athos. Most publishers, however, appear to believe that readers expect accounts to be either sources of information (guidebooks) or entertainment (travel writing). In republishing a series of nineteenth century books, Archaeopress views tourists as carrying a range of different texts, rather than an all-purpose account: "*3rdguides* offer the more dedicated traveller a range of classic, personal accounts . . . to pack along with the general and cultural guides you'll also need" (Wordsworth 2004: cover).

By the 1970s and '80s, visitors to Greece were much more diverse in their social and financial backgrounds than travellers of the immediate post-war period. Roger Bray has discussed how, from the 1950s onwards, factors such as education, increased earnings, and television, brought the possibility as well as the aspiration for foreign travel to new sections of the British people (Bray and Raitz 2001:23). Package holidays catered for those who lacked confidence in making their own arrangements in foreign countries, so that in the mid-1970s the managing director of the travel company Cosmos could state that the "working-class traveller has now become top dog" (Bray and Raitz 2001:196). Willy Russell's character Shirley Valentine, in his 1980s play of the same name, escaped to Greece from her role as a Liverpool housewife: "I'd allowed myself to live this little life when inside me there was so much" (Russell 1988:30). But some still chose Greece for residency because of its cultural associations. In the 1980s, Austen Kark was seeking a "retirement home with a difference. Infinite heart's ease with the wine-dark Aegean as back-drop and Homer (in translation) as companion" (Kark 1994:40). Likewise, when Emma Tennant explained what had compelled her to live in *A House in Corfu*, a classical reference was not far from her mind.

> Anyone wanting to up sticks and move a thousand miles, to a country where a foreign language is spoken and the local customs are in need of strict observance, must be so filled with wonder by the place that they are, like Odysseus as he approaches Circe's island, incapable of stopping themselves from anchoring there. (Tennant 2002:24)

Some writers have continued to describe the Greeks they encounter as resembling ancient people. Youths on the beach remind Sofka Zinovieff of "figures on Greek vases; reckless Icarus about to fly too close to the sun" (2004:247). Eleni Gage's four aunts "fulfil the same function" as a Greek theatrical chorus (2004:16). Yet such thoughts are on the wane. As I mentioned in chapter two, changing priorities and structures had profound consequences for the level and nature of knowledge about the classical world imparted through formal education in Britain. As John Bulwer explains, from the 1970s onwards

> Classics was squeezed out of the curriculum of the timetable of the comprehensive schools by a mixture of pressure from other subjects, a tendency to modernisation and even political opposition. (2006:126)

In recent years the academic community has attempted to reintroduce Classics into the curriculum of mainstream schools through such initiatives as the *Minimus* Latin project for children aged between seven and ten (Bulwer 2006:129). It must also be true that, as Bulwer suggests (2006:131), those who currently choose to study the ancient past at school or university are more committed than many of the pupils forced to decline Latin and Greek in the early decades of the last century.

Nevertheless, the old certainties about the British and their knowledge of classical culture have gone. Writers can no longer introduce minor literary figures, or even the giants of history such as Thucydides or Herodotus, into their travel narratives without explanation. Asked about *Greece*, British people would be more likely to summon up the tourist pleasures of "sun and sea" than the concept of democracy. Yet some conventional representations of Greece and the Greeks have shown a remarkable tenacity and survive into today's literature. The hospitality of the Greeks continues to be saluted, though now severed from thoughts of being a Homeric or classical survival. Instead, Anthony Cox writes of a people "devoid of the forced niceties of so much English behaviour and [who] were warm, spontaneous, open and expressive" (2001:9).

In the mid-twentieth century, Greece was seen as a country of the past. Now, Eleni Gage is able to encounter a "shepherd woman chatting away on a cellphone" (Gage, E. 2004:42). Indeed, a British newspaper recently reported that a shepherd, having taken refuge in a tree, was saved from marauding wolves by phoning his brother (*Times* 2002). Such technological developments fuel literary predictions that the "traditional" Greece is about to disappear, despite the fact that changes wrought by tourism and modernization were being criticized sixty years ago. As early as 1946, in a letter to T. S. Eliot, Lawrence Durrell had recognized that British writers were implicated in this process of change: "I fear we have done Greece harm by all the propaganda we've done for it these years.

Everyone wants to go there now" (1969:83). In 2004 John Mole had found "timeless, rural Greece", yet he contributed to its demise by exhorting readers to "catch it before it goes" (2004: cover). Likewise, Terry Cook fears that what he calls the "real" Greece is "disappearing fast under the crass and pointless rubbish of modern society" (Cook and Cook 2006:5). However Michael Saunders argues that such apparent transformations are superficial.

> Despite technologies bringing more material luxuries to the village, the same sense of values remain. Friendship, conviviality and kindness still flourish, as they always did. (Saunders 2005:94)

The writer whose work most frequently challenges traditional British responses to "timeless" Greece is Roger Jinkinson. His 2005 *Tales from a Greek Island* tells the familiar story of a Westerner escaping to rural life abroad. Jinkinson asks readers to examine whether their ways of dealing with life and death are really so much better than the apparently strange traditions of the Greeks (2005:80), and this is rendered more than mere rhetoric by his willingness to reappraise other assumptions and actions of Westerners. For example, he criticizes anthropologists for reducing a "living culture into something dry and segmented" (2005:136). Jinkinson consistently allies himself with the attitudes of the locals—writing of "*our* children", for example—and he is proud to be regarded as a villager rather than a tourist (2005:5, 18, my emphasis). The adoption by resident writers of a superior status to other travellers is hardly a new phenomenon. But Jinkinson's tirade against the portrayal of Greeks as "caricatures" and his insistence that Greek culture is "evolving" rather than "timeless" (2005:136, 170), is at the very least refreshing. It may be more, and point to new possibilities for the writing of Greece and its people.

Jinkinson is derogatory about package trips in which tourists are offered "an authentic experience" of mountain villages, and return with "their authentic souvenirs and their authentic memories" (2005:136). As in other parts of the world, searching for the "authentic Greece" has always been to chase the chimera. In the early 1970s Jean Robertson and Duncan Gardiner pursued "a typical Cretan, whom we spent a surreptitious half hour trying to photograph and who turned out to have spent fifty years in America" (1972:7). As Anthony Cox points out, whether one finds "authenticity" depends on how it is defined.

> Greek towns and villages in themselves could often grow to be hideously ugly, without any outside help, while remaining completely "unspoilt" as

genuine communities in which newcomers would find friendship and
good-neighbourliness. (Cox 2001:32)

Travellers are often informed by guidebooks that the "real" Greece is
where Greeks—not tourists—eat and socialise. A recent edition of the
Blue Guide to Athens, for example, advised that "it is best always to
choose establishments crowded with locals" (Barber, R. 2002: 34). But in
the Greece of today that is as likely, in urbanised parts at least, to be an
outlet of a global fast food chain as a "traditional" Greek taverna.

CONCLUSION

At the beginning of the 1990s, in a landmark study, Mary Louise Pratt criticized other analyses of travel writing as merely "celebratory" or "documentary" (1992:10). Less than ten years later, however, Ángel Quintana was able to comment that it was an "already commonplace assumption" among cultural historians that travel texts "are often more revealing about the culture of the traveller than about that of the places and people visited" (2001:173). Yet this has not filtered through to studies of travel writing about Greece, which all too often consist of an uncomplicated quarrying of texts for amusing anecdote or allegedly accurate information about the contemporary "state" of the country. This, regrettably, is essentially the approach taken by the contributors to a recent slim volume from the Classical Association devoted to *Travellers to Greece* (Stray 2006). Tony Brothers, for example, quotes James Stuart and Nicholas Revett as experiencing "insolent rapacity" from the Greek who served as British Consul in Athens during their visit of the 1700s (Stray 2006:11). Yet Brothers elects not to explore the reasons why the travellers' characterization of this individual may have arisen. In the same volume, Brenda Stones claims to be "discussing" the late nineteenth century writings of Mabel Bent (Stray 2006:22). In truth, however, Stones' work is largely restricted to summarization and quotation, with very little consideration of the influences upon Bent's representation of Greece.

In this book my intention has been to show the complexity and value of travel writing about Greece. Much of the material I have discussed may be regarded as of little literary merit, but it forms an archive of attitudes, offering opportunities to explore the relationship between the present and the past, and between Britain and Greece. Travel writing should be investigated and approached from a number of angles. For chapters three and four I used a system of textual analysis to establish themes in the representation of a particular foreign country within and across a number of travel narratives. But it is only (as I did in chapters one and two) by examining other discourses—historical and sociological, as well as literary—that we can reach an understanding of how these representations came to be formed.

During the three decades following the Second World War, most travel narratives contained a Greek people with positive attributes, attitudes and behaviour. It was rare to find a writer venturing so sweeping a criticism as Patrick Anderson.

> Much of the population is big-hipped, fat-bottomed and as interminably, brightly narcissistic and insensitive (those hair-combings and paintings of the co-respondent shoes) as any marcelled hair-stylist in hell. (1963:95)

Most, however, appeared "in love with the Greeks" (Osler 1957:144). As with nineteenth century travellers, "the world of antiquity was not the unknown but the familiar" (Galani-Moutafi 2000:209). Therefore, when travelling in the modern country called Greece, the past was ever present as a comparison. Ian MacNiven's comment about *Prospero's Cell* seems applicable to many other works of travel writing of that period: Lawrence Durrell saw "the present in the mirror of the past" (MacNiven 1998:308). Greece was not, of course, the only country in which travellers' perceptions were shaped by history. Sharon Ouditt has written that George Gissing's journey in Italy was "illuminated as much by his imagination as by the physical landscapes in front of him, and those landscapes are populated as much by the dead as the living" (2006:134). But in Italy there were stronger competing influences on visitors: the pull of that later flowering of culture, the Renaissance, and the power of the Roman Catholic Church. In Greece, later history was generally thought by travellers to be immaterial and its legacy unimportant.

The journey to Greece was imagined to involve temporal as well as physical travel. Greece offered an opportunity not merely to view the birthplace of Western culture, but to journey back and experience the more fulfilling lifestyle of a simpler age. Travellers of the 1950s onwards were rejecting "the rat-race of modern commercialism" (Clift 1959:19). They claimed to encounter a people whose way of life had remained unchanged for an often unspecified number of centuries. This assumption, as we have seen, proved extremely useful for anthropologists of the post-war period, who desired to find primitiveness on their doorstep. Anthropological studies invariably portrayed the Greeks as the exotic element within Europe. Greece was found to be simultaneously familiar and alien. The connection with the classical past (which aided the perception of the Greeks as European) had been problematic as early as the nineteenth century.

> Modern Greece became the heir of ancient Greece, and classical heritage
> became the means through which the Greeks could come closer to their
> European counterparts. On the other hand, it was this same heritage that
> reminded the West of how different contemporary Greeks were from their
> classical ancestors. (Yalouri 2001:187)

Travel writers of the 1940s onwards were unable to find the heights of
civilization attained in the ancient world—art, architecture, poetry,
plays—in a modern nation that had recently experienced a devastating war
(not to mention earlier centuries under the Turkish yoke), and was thus not
a wealthy, modern country like Britain. In this way, "modern" Greece
could be regarded both as the birthplace of European culture and as a
primitive backwater. This left the heirs of the classical tradition as those
(in Western Europe) who had carried on where the Greeks of the classical
period had left off.

The sites and monuments too were separated from the normal flow of
time. A visit to the ruins of the Acropolis was seen not to benefit from
association with the modern city of Athens, which was experiencing rapid
growth and change in the post-war period. Instead, the surroundings of the
rock were usually ignored or denigrated. Sir Patrick Leigh Fermor, the
elder statesman of travel writers about Greece, has written of his desire to
view the Acropolis at an earlier time: "the wish to be lifted by magic to an
earlier city, before the fumes of today had driven the Caryatids from their
plinth, after twenty-three hundred years" (Leigh Fermor 2003:245).[12] This
left the remains of the past disconnected from the present, seen as timeless
wonders set apart from the traffic, noise and unpleasantness. The
Acropolis monuments became symbols: of ancient Athens, the whole of
the classical past, Western culture, and human achievement in general. At
many other sites in Greece, however, the focus of the travel writer's
attention was literary or historical association rather than aesthetics. Here,
the presence and effect of the surroundings was more often acknowledged
to be part of the experience than was the case at the Acropolis. At
Mycenae and Delphi, for example, the respectively brooding and awe
inspiring landscapes could be made to reflect the ancient events that had
led to those locations being regarded as significant by the mid-twentieth
century traveller. However, these sites were still seen as separate from the
modern world, since the landscapes in which they were situated were
described as being "natural", not shaped by the effects of modernity.
Writers even felt able to use such ruins as vehicles for "time travel", to
escape the present.

Travel writers' perceptions of the sites and monuments as untouched by later developments were aided by the campaigns of excavation and restoration which had been conducted in Greece from the early nineteenth century onwards. The physical changes wrought by Ottoman rule were suppressed in post-independence Greece. Instead, as I have discussed, there was the systematic promotion of the past which would find favour with elites both within the country and in Western Europe. The history of Greece was written as going straight from the Roman Empire to nineteenth century independence. Physically as well as mentally then, travellers saw a Greece which accorded with their beliefs about the significance of that country to Western culture. Travel writers may have felt that ruins allowed them to get closer to antiquity than they could achieve merely through reading literature or history at home. However, even as they found the classical past in the present, travel writers were conscious that antiquity was not fully accessible. Stepping into history required the use of the travellers' imaginations, and some sites were so ruinous as to defeat their abilities. In their encounters with the Greek people and the physical remains, travellers found only relics of the ancient past: fragments not the whole.

I have shown that, especially during the mid-twentieth century, conventional representations existed in the work of travel writers. I would not, however, argue that their portrayal of Greece was necessarily synonymous with the view held by most Britons. It may have been the case that there was a near-universal opinion in the 1940s. Wartime propaganda, including that which masqueraded as travel writing, emphasised the honest endeavour, heroism, generosity, and strength of democratic sentiment, of the Greek people. Links were posited with their classical forebears, with whom the British were imagined to have more of an acquaintance than the modern Greeks. The latter were "to all but a fraction of Western Europeans, an unknown people" (Powell 1941:61). However, I would suggest that British perceptions are likely to have significantly diversified from the 1960s onwards. Writers and publishers were as uncertain as modern scholars are about the extent to which the "general public" of that period was conversant with the details of the classical past, especially at a time of sweeping changes to formal education. Certainly, there was a widening gap between the background of the writers themselves and the majority of those who were visiting Greece. The latter were not now those who could afford to make a relatively long, expensive journey to visit cultural sights, but tourists in search of sun and sea. At the time I write this, far fewer Britons than was the case half a century ago would feel affinity with ancient Greece and its cultural heritage.

Every country has its stereotypes, and every country has its role for the outsider as the antithesis or "other" of the home. For British observers and participants, Greece was—and is—a fantasy land, in which notions of past and present, civilization and culture, timelessness and change, could be played out. In much of travel writing, this was theme park Greece, welcoming but slightly unfamiliar. As with all perceptions and representations of the "other", the reality of Greece in the twentieth century was always more complex than travel writers showed. But it is the *selections* made when constructing travel narratives which provide insights into what it was that travellers, writers and readers imagined and desired of Greece and its people. As travel to Greece—actual and through reading literature—reaches new levels of popularity, it is certain that Greek myths will continue.

APPENDIX A

ACCOUNTS OF TRAVEL TO GREECE PUBLISHED IN BRITAIN, 1940-1974[13]

Adams, Phoebe-Lou. 1965. *A Rough Map of Greece*. London: Hutchinson.

Anderson, Patrick. 1958. *First Steps in Greece*. London: Chatto and Windus.

—. 1963. *Dolphin Days: A Writer's Notebook on Mediterranean Pleasures*. London: Gollancz.

Andrews, Kevin. 1959. *The Flight of Ikaros: A Journey into Greece*. London: Weidenfeld and Nicolson.

Balfour, Patrick. 1951. *The Orphaned Realm: Journeys in Cyprus*. London: Percival Marshall.

Bell, Robert. 1961. *By Road to Greece*. London: Alvin Redman.

Braddock, Joseph. 1967. *Some Greek Islands: The Shores of Light*. London: Robert Hale.

—. 1970. *Sappho's Island: A Paean for Lesbos*. London: Constable.

Brockway, Lucile, and George Brockway. 1966. *Greece: A Classical Tour with Extras*. London: Gollancz.

Brook, Ian. 1971. *A Sea Blue Boat, and a Sun God's Island*. London: Adland Coles.

Bull, Peter. 1967. *It Isn't All Greek to Me*. London: Peter Davies.

Carroll, Michael. 1965. *Gates of the Wind*. London: John Murray.

Causton, Jack, ed. 1972. *Skiathos: The Shaded Isle*. Send, Surrey: The Cartbridge Press.

Chamberlain, Brenda. 1965. *A Rope of Vines: Journal from a Greek Island*. London: Hodder and Stoughton.

Clift, Charmian. 1958. *Mermaid Singing*. London: Michael Joseph.

—. 1959. *Peel me a Lotus*. London: Hutchinson.

Coles, S. F. A. 1965. *Greece: A Journey in Time*. London: Robert Hale.

Dodge, David. 1955. *Talking Turkey*. London: Arthur Barker.

Durrell, Gerald. 1959. *My Family and Other Animals*. Harmondsworth: Penguin.

Durrell, Lawrence. 1945. *Prospero's Cell*. London: Faber.

—. 1953. *Reflections on a Marine Venus: A Companion to the Landscape of Rhodes*. London: Faber.

—. 1957. *Bitter Lemons of Cyprus*. London: Faber.

Duxbury, Ken. 1973. *Lugworm on the Loose: Exploring Greece in an Open Dinghy*. London: Pelham.

Elliot, W. R. 1971. *Monemvasia: The Gibraltar of Greece*. London: Dennis Dobson.

Evans, Stanley. 1965. *In Evening Dress to Calvary: A Few Days in Palestine and Greece*. London: S. C. M.

Fielding, Xan. 1953. *The Stronghold: An Account of the Four Seasons in the White Mountains of Crete*. London: Secker and Warburg.

Finer, Leslie. 1964. *Passport to Greece*. London: Longmans.

Forbes, Duncan. 1970. *The Heart of Greece*. London: Robert Hale.

Forbes-Boyd, Eric. 1965. *In Crusader Greece*. London: Centaur.

—. 1970. *Aegean Quest: A Search for Venetian Greece*. London: Dent.

Forte, John Knox, ed. 1964. *Corfu: Venus of the Isles*. East Essex Gazette.

Foss, Arthur. 1969. *The Ionian Islands*. London: Faber.

Golding, Louis. 1955. *Goodbye to Ithaca*. London: Hutchinson.

Golding, William. 1965. *The Hot Gates, and Other Occasional Pieces*. London: Faber.

Hogarth, Paul. 1953. *Defiant People*. London: Lawrence and Wishart.

Hughes, Hilda, ed. 1944. *The Glory that is Greece*. London: Hutchinson.

John, Evan. 1954. *Time after Earthquake: An Adventure Among Greek Islands in August, 1953*. London: Heinemann.

Kanelli, Sheelagh. 1965. *Earth and Water: A Marriage into Greece*. London: Hodder and Stoughton.

Kimbrough, Emily. 1957. *Water, Water Everywhere*. London: Heinemann.

—. 1965. *Forever Old, Forever New*. London: Heinemann.

Kininmonth, Christopher. 1949. *The Children of Thetis: A Study of Islands and Islanders in the Aegean*. London: John Lehmann.

Knowles, John. 1964. *Double Vision: American Thoughts Abroad*. London: Secker and Warburg.

Krippner, Monica. 1957. *Beyond Athens: Journeys Through Greece*. London: Geoffrey Bles.

Kubly, Herbert. 1970. *Gods and Heroes*. London: Gollancz.

Lancaster, Osbert. 1947. *Classical Landscape with Figures*. London: John Murray.

Lee, C. P. 1957. *Athenian Adventure: With Alarums and Excursions*. London: Gollancz.

Lee, Laurie, and Ralph Keene. 1947. *We Made a Film in Cyprus*. London: Longmans.

Leigh Fermor, Patrick. 1958. *Mani: Travels in the Southern Peloponnese.*
    Reprint, Harmondsworth: Penguin, 1984.
—. 1966. *Roumeli: Travels in Northern Greece.* London: John Murray.
Liddell, Robert. 1954. *Aegean Greece.* London: Jonathan Cape.
—. 1958. *The Morea.* London: Jonathan Cape.
—. 1965. *Mainland Greece.* London: Longmans.
Loch, Joice NanKivell. 1968. *A Fringe of Blue.* London: John Murray.
Mackenzie, Compton. 1960. *Greece in My Life.* London: Chatto and
    Windus.
Mais, S. P. B. and Gillian Mais. 1962. *Greek Holiday.* London: Alvin
    Redman.
Matthews, Carola. 1968. *The Mad Pomegranate Tree: An Image of
    Modern Greece.* London: Macmillan.
—. 1971. *At the Top of the Muletrack.* London: Macmillan.
Mayne, Peter. 1958. *The Private Sea.* London: John Murray.
Mikes, George. 1965. *Eureka! Rummaging in Greece.* London: Andre
    Deutsch.
Miller, Henry. 1942. *The Colossus of Maroussi.* Reprint, London:
    Minerva, 1991.
Morpurgo, J. E. 1963. *The Road to Athens.* London: Eyre and
    Spottiswoode.
Napier, Malcolm. 1972. *An Anthology.* London: Regency Press.
Osler, Michael. 1957. *Journey to Hattusas.* London: Hutchinson.
Patmore, Derek. 1944. *Images of Greece.* London: Country Life.
Payne, Robert. 1961. *The Splendour of Greece.* London: Robert Hale.
—. 1965. *The Isles of Greece.* London: Hamish Hamilton.
Pierson, John H. G. 1973. *Island in Greece.* London: The Mitre Press.
Pollard, John. 1955. *Journey to the Styx.* London: Christopher Johnson.
Powell, Dilys. 1941. *Remember Greece.* London: Hodder and Stoughton.
—. 1957. *An Affair of the Heart.* London: Hodder and Stoughton.
—. 1973. *The Villa Ariadne.* London: Hodder and Stoughton.
Roland, Betty. 1963. *Lesbos: The Pagan Island.* London: Angus and
    Robertson.
Robertson, Jean, and Duncan Gardiner. 1972. *Twelve Days in Crete.*
    London: Times Newspapers.
Sansom, William. 1968. *Grand Tour Today.* London: Hogarth Press.
Schildt, Goran. 1953. *In the Wake of Odysseus.* Translated from the
    Swedish by Alan Blair. London: Staples.
Simpson, Colin. 1969. *Greece: The Unclouded Eye.* London: Hodder and
    Stoughton.

Smith, Ashley. 1948. *Greece: Moments of Grace*. London: Eyre and Spottiswood.

Smith, Michael Llewellyn. 1965. *The Great Island: A Study of Crete*. London: Longmans.

Spain, Nancy. 1964. *A Funny Thing Happened on the Way*. London: Hutchinson.

Stark, Freya. 1956. *The Lycian Shore: Along the Coast of Turkey by Yacht*. Reprint, London: Century, 1989.

—. 1969. *Space, Time and Movement in Landscape*. London: privately printed.

Sykes, John. 1965. *Caïque: A Portrait of Greek Islanders*. London: Hutchinson.

Thurston, Hazel. 1960. *From Darkest Mum*. London: Chapman and Hall.

Toulmin, Stephen. 1963. *Night Sky at Rhodes*. London: Methuen.

Toy, Barbara. 1970. *Rendezvous in Cyprus*. London: John Murray.

Travis, William. 1970. *Bus Stop Symi*. London: Rapp and Whiting.

Tremayne, Penelope. 1958. *Below the Tide*. London: Hutchinson.

Vyvyan, C. C. 1955. *Temples and Flowers: A Journey to Greece*. London: Peter Owen.

Warner, Rex. 1950. *Views of Attica and its Surroundings*. London: John Lehmann.

Whelpton, Barbara. 1954. *A Window on Greece*. London: Heinemann.

Whelpton, Eric, and Barbara Whelpton. 1961. *Greece and the Islands*. London: The Travel Book Club.

Wigram, W. A. 1947. *Hellenic Travel*. London: Faber.

APPENDIX B

ACCOUNTS OF TRAVEL TO GREECE PUBLISHED IN BRITAIN, 1940-1974 (ORGANISED BY DECADE)[14]

1940-49

Durrell, Lawrence. 1945. *Prospero's Cell*. London: Faber.
Hughes, Hilda, ed. 1944. *The Glory that is Greece*. London: Hutchinson.
Kininmonth, Christopher. 1949. *The Children of Thetis: A Study of Islands and Islanders in the Aegean*. London: John Lehmann.
Lancaster, Osbert. 1947. *Classical Landscape with Figures*. London: John Murray.
Lee, Laurie, and Ralph Keene. 1947. *We Made a Film in Cyprus*. London: Longmans.
Miller, Henry. 1942. *The Colossus of Maroussi*. Reprint, London: Minerva, 1991.
Patmore, Derek. 1944. *Images of Greece*. London: Country Life.
Powell, Dilys. 1941. *Remember Greece*. London: Hodder and Stoughton.
Smith, Ashley. 1948. *Greece: Moments of Grace*. London: Eyre and Spottiswood.
Wigram, W. A. 1947. *Hellenic Travel*. London: Faber.

1950-59

Anderson, Patrick. 1958. *First Steps in Greece*. London: Chatto and Windus.
Andrews, Kevin. 1959. *The Flight of Ikaros: A Journey into Greece*. London: Weidenfeld and Nicolson.
Balfour, Patrick. 1951. *The Orphaned Realm: Journeys in Cyprus*. London: Percival Marshall.
Clift, Charmian. 1958. *Mermaid Singing*. London: Michael Joseph.
—. 1959. *Peel me a Lotus*. London: Hutchinson.

Dodge, David. 1955. *Talking Turkey*. London: Arthur Barker.

Durrell, Gerald. 1959. *My Family and Other Animals*. Harmondsworth: Penguin.

Durrell, Lawrence. 1953. *Reflections on a Marine Venus: A Companion to the Landscape of Rhodes*. London: Faber.

—. 1957. *Bitter Lemons of Cyprus*. London: Faber.

Fielding, Xan. 1953. *The Stronghold: An Account of the Four Seasons in the White Mountains of Crete*. London: Secker and Warburg.

Golding, Louis. 1955. *Goodbye to Ithaca*. London: Hutchinson.

Hogarth, Paul. 1953. *Defiant People*. London: Lawrence and Wishart.

John, Evan. 1954. *Time after Earthquake: An Adventure Among Greek Islands in August, 1953*. London: Heinemann.

Kimbrough, Emily. 1957. *Water, Water Everywhere*. London: Heinemann.

Krippner, Monica. 1957. *Beyond Athens: Journeys Through Greece*. London: Geoffrey Bles.

Lee, C. P. 1957. *Athenian Adventure: With Alarums and Excursions*. London: Gollancz.

Leigh Fermor, Patrick. 1958. *Mani: Travels in the Southern Peloponnese*. Reprint, Harmondsworth: Penguin, 1984.

Liddell, Robert. 1954. *Aegean Greece*. London: Jonathan Cape.

—. 1958. *The Morea*. London: Jonathan Cape.

Mayne, Peter. 1958. *The Private Sea*. London: John Murray.

Osler, Michael. 1957. *Journey to Hattusas*. London: Hutchinson.

Pollard, John. 1955. *Journey to the Styx*. London: Christopher Johnson.

Powell, Dilys. 1957. *An Affair of the Heart*. London: Hodder and Stoughton.

Schildt, Goran. 1953. *In the Wake of Odysseus*. Translated from the Swedish by Alan Blair. London: Staples.

Stark, Freya. 1956. *The Lycian Shore: Along the Coast of Turkey by Yacht*. Reprint, London: Century, 1989.

Tremayne, Penelope. 1958. *Below the Tide*. London: Hutchinson.

Vyvyan, C. C. 1955. *Temples and Flowers: A Journey to Greece*. London: Peter Owen.

Warner, Rex. 1950. *Views of Attica and its Surroundings*. London: John Lehmann.

Whelpton, Barbara. 1954. *A Window on Greece*. London: Heinemann.

1960-74

Adams, Phoebe-Lou. 1965. *A Rough Map of Greece*. London: Hutchinson.

Anderson, Patrick. 1963. *Dolphin Days: A Writer's Notebook on Mediterranean Pleasures*. London: Gollancz.

Bell, Robert. 1961. *By Road to Greece*. London: Alvin Redman.

Braddock, Joseph. 1967. *Some Greek Islands: The Shores of Light*. London: Robert Hale.

—. 1970. *Sappho's Island: A Paean for Lesbos*. London: Constable.

Brockway, Lucile, and George Brockway. 1966. *Greece: A Classical Tour with Extras*. London: Gollancz.

Brook, Ian. 1971. *A Sea Blue Boat, and a Sun God's Island*. London: Adland Coles.

Bull, Peter. 1967. *It Isn't All Greek to Me*. London: Peter Davies.

Carroll, Michael. 1965. *Gates of the Wind*. London: John Murray.

Causton, Jack, ed. 1972. *Skiathos: The Shaded Isle*. Send, Surrey: The Cartbridge Press.

Chamberlain, Brenda. 1965. *A Rope of Vines: Journal from a Greek Island*. London: Hodder and Stoughton.

Coles, S. F. A. 1965. *Greece: A Journey in Time*. London: Robert Hale.

Duxbury, Ken. 1973. *Lugworm on the Loose: Exploring Greece in an Open Dinghy*. London: Pelham.

Elliot, W. R. 1971. *Monemvasia: The Gibraltar of Greece*. London: Dennis Dobson.

Evans, Stanley. 1965. *In Evening Dress to Calvary: A Few Days in Palestine and Greece*. London: S. C. M.

Finer, Leslie. 1964. *Passport to Greece*. London: Longmans.

Forbes, Duncan. 1970. *The Heart of Greece*. London: Robert Hale.

Forbes-Boyd, Eric. 1965. *In Crusader Greece*. London: Centaur.

—. 1970. *Aegean Quest: A Search for Venetian Greece*. London: Dent.

Forte, John Knox, ed. 1964. *Corfu: Venus of the Isles*. East Essex Gazette.

Foss, Arthur. 1969. *The Ionian Islands*. London: Faber.

Golding, William. 1965. *The Hot Gates, and Other Occasional Pieces*. London: Faber.

Kanelli, Sheelagh. 1965. *Earth and Water: A Marriage into Greece*. London: Hodder and Stoughton.

Kimbrough, Emily. 1965. *Forever Old, Forever New*. London: Heinemann.

Knowles, John. 1964. *Double Vision: American Thoughts Abroad*. London: Secker and Warburg.

Kubly, Herbert. 1970. *Gods and Heroes*. London: Gollancz.

Leigh Fermor, Patrick. 1966. *Roumeli: Travels in Northern Greece*. London: John Murray.

Liddell, Robert. 1965. *Mainland Greece*. London: Longmans.

Loch, Joice NanKivell. 1968. *A Fringe of Blue*. London: John Murray.

Mackenzie, Compton. 1960. *Greece in My Life*. London: Chatto and Windus.

Mais, S. P. B. and Gillian Mais. 1962. *Greek Holiday*. London: Alvin Redman.

Matthews, Carola. 1968. *The Mad Pomegranate Tree: An Image of Modern Greece*. London: Macmillan.

—. 1971. *At the Top of the Muletrack*. London: Macmillan.

Mikes, George. 1965. *Eureka! Rummaging in Greece*. London: Andre Deutsch.

Morpurgo, J. E. 1963. *The Road to Athens*. London: Eyre and Spottiswoode.

Napier, Malcolm. 1972. *An Anthology*. London: Regency Press.

Payne, Robert. 1961. *The Splendour of Greece*. London: Robert Hale.

—. 1965. *The Isles of Greece*. London: Hamish Hamilton.

Pierson, John H. G. 1973. *Island in Greece*. London: The Mitre Press.

Powell, Dilys. 1973. *The Villa Ariadne*. London: Hodder and Stoughton.

Robertson, Jean, and Duncan Gardiner. 1972. *Twelve Days in Crete*. London: Times Newspapers.

Roland, Betty. 1963. *Lesbos: The Pagan Island*. London: Angus and Robertson.

Sansom, William. 1968. *Grand Tour Today*. London: Hogarth Press.

Simpson, Colin. 1969. *Greece: The Unclouded Eye*. London: Hodder and Stoughton.

Smith, Michael Llewellyn. 1965. *The Great Island: A Study of Crete*. London: Longmans.

Spain, Nancy. 1964. *A Funny Thing Happened on the Way*. London: Hutchinson.

Stark, Freya. 1969. *Space, Time and Movement in Landscape*. London: privately printed.

Sykes, John. 1965. *Caïque: A Portrait of Greek Islanders*. London: Hutchinson.

Thurston, Hazel. 1960. *From Darkest Mum*. London: Chapman and Hall.

Toulmin, Stephen. 1963. *Night Sky at Rhodes*. London: Methuen.

Toy, Barbara. 1970. *Rendezvous in Cyprus*. London: John Murray.

Travis, William. 1970. *Bus Stop Symi*. London: Rapp and Whiting.

Whelpton, Eric, and Barbara Whelpton. 1961. *Greece and the Islands*. London: The Travel Book Club.

APPENDIX C

METHOD FOR ANALYSING TRAVEL TEXTS

Whilst much has been written about travel literature in recent years, remarkably little consideration has been given to how analysts should extract information from travel accounts and make generalisations about the representation of peoples and places within the genre. For many scholars, "I read all these" (as Norman Buchignani puts it; 2000:117) represents their statement of methodology. Tim Youngs, in his book about travel writing on Africa, is by no means unusual in that he discusses his choice of travel accounts on the basis of their date, authors, and geographical area, but makes little attempt to outline his methodology for the reading of those texts (Youngs 1994:7). In a paper published in the inaugural issue of the academic journal *Journeys*, Norman Buchignani roundly criticized other scholars of travel writing for their failure to justify

> how analytical assertions are representative of the texts and larger discourses they are meant to represent . . . Sampling procedures are almost never explained, either in regard to how particular texts are drawn from a larger discourse, or quotes are derived from a single text. (Buchignani 2000:118)

Buchignani proposed a novel approach to the analysis of travel texts based on "the consistent application of fieldwork-derived methodological standards and practice" (2000:114). He took at his case study the texts published up to 1850 which mentioned the South African people called Hottentots. He presented graphs and spreadsheets showing the number of travellers who attached certain characteristics to Hottentots during each twenty year period from 1497 to 1850. From this, Buchignani was able to reach conclusions about the frequency of different "topical domains" and about how these were used in conjunction with each other. For example, it can be said that between 1652 and 1720 laziness "is the most commonly mentioned personal or moral characteristic then assigned to Hottentots", and Buchignani was also able to identify "the topical domains most commonly found in the same paragraph as laziness" (2000:131, 139).

Thus Buchignani aimed to leave an "audit trail" showing how his analytical conclusions were linked to data gathered from the travel literature (2000:125, and note 16).

For the period which forms the central concern of this book, 1940-1974, themes used for the representation of Greece have been identified and tracked using a system of analysis inspired by Buchignani. Each travel book published at that time (see appendices A and B) was considered in the light of a series of attributes or characteristics of the sites and monuments and the Greek people. The results are shown below in tables 1-7.

In tables 1-4, the following categories or attributes are employed with reference to descriptions of ancient Greek sites and monuments:
A) praised for aesthetics of building;
B) praised for aesthetics of setting;
C) praised for total aesthetic effect of building/monument and its setting;
D) denigrated for aesthetics of building;
E) denigrated for aesthetics of setting;
F) denigrated for aesthetic effect of building/monument and its setting;
G) said to have created *mood* in observer;
H) said to have given observer direct link with past;
I) easy to recreate original appearance in the observer's mind;
J) difficult/unable to recreate original appearance in the observer's mind;
K) useful as archaeological evidence for ancient life;
L) site confirms or denies information found in ancient texts;
M) ancient accounts or information external to the site help to make sense of remains viewed;
N) reference to or quotation from ancient author;
O) reference to or quotation from modern traveller;
P) specific historical/mythological information about site given.

In each of tables 1-4 the number of texts which contain a description (however brief) of a site or monument is shown next to its name at the top of the column. This is expressed in tables 1-3 as a percentage of the total texts within each decade (with the actual number in square brackets) or, in table 4, across the period as a whole. The figures for the categories A-P are then shown as a percentage of the number of texts that refer to this site, with the figure in square brackets being the actual number. For example, in table 1 it can be seen that 20% of texts produced during the 1940s (i.e. 2

of 10) describe Aegina; of these, 100% (i.e. 2) praise the aesthetics of the Temple of Aphaia (category A).

The Mirror of Antiquity: 20th Century British Travellers in Greece

Table 1. Ancient sites and monuments in travel writing, 1940–49

	Aegina	Athens (Acropolis)	Bassae	Corinth	Crete	Delphi	Mycenae	Olympia	Sounion	Sparta
	20 [2]	70 [7]	40 [4]	30 [3]	50 [5]	60 [6]	50 [5]	50 [5]	40 [4]	10 [1]
A	100 [2]	86 [6]	25 [1]		20 [1]	33 [2]	40 [2]	40 [2]	25 [1]	
B	100 [2]	29 [2]	25 [1]		20 [1]	50 [3]	20 [1]	40 [2]		100 [1]
C	50 [1]	14 [1]	50 [2]					40 [2]	50 [2]	
D		14 [1]		33 [1]					50 [2]	
E										
F							20 [1]			
G	50 [1]				20 [1]	17 [1]	20 [1]			
H		29 [2]				17 [1]				
I					60 [3]	17 [1]	20 [1]			
J					20 [1]	17 [1]	20 [1]			
K					40 [2]		20 [1]			
L				33 [1]	20 [1]		20 [1]	20 [1]		
M							20 [1]			
N	50 [1]	29 [2]	50 [2]	33 [1]	20 [1]	17 [1]	40 [2]			100 [1]
O			25 [1]	33 [1]				20 [1]	25 [1]	
P	100 [2]	29 [2]	25 [1]	67 [2]	40 [2]	67 [4]	60 [3]	40 [2]		100 [1]

Appendix C

Table 2. Ancient sites and monuments in travel writing, 1950-59

	Aegina	Athens (Acropolis)	Bassae	Corinth	Crete	Delphi	Mycenae	Olympia	Sounion	Sparta
	14 [4]	48 [14]	7 [2]	24 [7]	24 [7]	38 [11]	38 [11]	14 [4]	28 [8]	24 [7]
A	25 [1]	57 [8]	100 [2]	43 [3]	29 [2]	55 [6]	36 [4]	50 [2]	63 [5]	43 [3]
B	50 [2]	21 [3]	100 [2]	57 [4]	29 [2]	73 [8]	55 [6]	100 [4]	13 [1]	14 [1]
C	75 [3]	79 [11]	50 [1]	43 [3]		64 [7]	36 [4]	25 [1]	38 [3]	29 [2]
D		7 [1]	50 [1]	14 [1]	29 [2]	9 [1]	9 [1]	25 [1]	13 [1]	14 [1]
E	25 [1]	36 [5]		14 [1]	14 [1]					
F		7 [1]								
G			50 [1]			36 [4]	55 [6]	25 [1]		
H		7 [1]				9 [1]	9 [1]			
I					29 [2]	9 [1]		25 [1]		
J					29 [2]	9 [1]		25[1]		
K				29 [2]	14 [1]		18 [2]			14 [1]
L					14 [1]		9 [1]			
M							9 [1]			
N	25 [1]	7 [1]	100 [2]	29 [2]		18 [2]	27 [3]	50 [2]		29 [2]
O	50 [2]	14 [2]	100 [2]				9 [1]	25 [1]	63 [5]	14 [1]
P	50 [2]	36 [5]	100 [2]	57 [4]	86 [6]	100 [11]	73 [8]	75 [3]	63 [5]	57 [4]

The Mirror of Antiquity: 20th Century British Travellers in Greece

Table 3. Ancient sites and monuments in travel writing, 1960-74

	Aegina	Athens (Acropolis)	Bassae	Corinth	Crete	Delphi	Mycenae	Olympia	Sounion	Sparta
	21 [11]	43 [23]	13 [7]	21 [11]	26 [14]	43 [23]	38 [20]	34 [18]	34 [18]	11 [6]
A	45 [5]	78 [18]	29 [2]	9 [1]	14 [2]	39 [9]	10 [2]	11 [2]	44 [8]	
B	64 [7]	22 [5]	43 [3]	27 [3]	43 [6]	74 [17]	25 [5]	56 [10]	50 [9]	33 [2]
C	45 [5]	52 [12]	71 [5]	9 [1]	14 [2]	35 [8]	45 [9]	39 [7]	22 [4]	
D		9 [2]		9 [1]	14 [2]			17 [3]	11 [2]	17 [1]
E		9 [2]			7 [1]				11 [2]	50 [3]
F		4 [1]								17 [1]
G		17 [4]		9 [1]	14 [2]	30 [7]	30 [6]	22 [4]		
H	9 [1]				21 [3]	9 [2]	15 [3]	22 [4]		
I					43 [6]	13 [3]	15 [3]	17 [3]	11 [2]	17 [1]
J		9 [2]		18 [2]	50 [7]	17 [4]	15 [3]	17 [3]		
K				9 [1]	36 [5]		25 [5]			
L					14 [2]		10 [2]			
M				18 [2]			20 [4]			
N	36 [4]	13 [3]	14 [1]	36 [4]	21 [3]	39 [9]	20 [4]	17 [3]	6 [1]	33 [2]
O	27 [3]	26 [6]	29 [2]		29 [4]	9 [2]	25 [5]	11 [2]	33 [6]	
P	82 [9]	55 [11]	43 [3]	73 [8]	64 [9]	70 [16]	70 [14]	61 [11]	22 [4]	33 [2]

Appendix C

Table 4. Ancient sites and monuments in travel writing, 1940-74

	Aegina	Athens (Acropolis)	Bassae	Corinth	Crete	Delphi	Mycenae	Olympia	Sounion	Sparta
	18 [17]	48 [44]	14 [13]	23 [21]	30 [26]	43 [40]	39 [36]	29 [27]	33 [30]	15 [14]
A	47 [8]	73 [32]	39 [5]	19 [4]	19 [5]	43 [17]	17 [6]	15 [4]	47 [14]	
B	65 [11]	23 [10]	46 [6]	33 [7]	35 [9]	70 [28]	36 [13]	59 [16]	33 [10]	43 [6]
C	53 [9]	55 [24]	62 [8]	19 [4]	8 [2]	38 [15]	39 [14]	37 [10]	30 [9]	7 [1]
D		9 [4]	8 [1]	14 [3]	15 [4]	3 [1]	3 [1]	22 [6]	17 [5]	21 [3]
E	6 [1]	16 [7]		10 [2]	8 [2]				7 [2]	29 [4]
F		5 [2]					3 [1]			7 [1]
G	6 [1]	9 [4]	8 [1]		12 [3]	30 [12]	36 [13]	19 [5]		
H	6 [1]	7 [3]			12 [3]	10 [4]	11 [4]	19 [5]		
I				10 [2]	42 [11]	13 [5]	8 [3]	15 [4]	7 [2]	7 [1]
J		5 [2]		14 [3]	38 [10]	15 [6]	17 [6]	15 [4]		
K				5 [1]	31 [8]		19 [7]			7 [1]
L				10 [2]	15 [4]		11 [4]	4 [1]		
M							19 [7]			
N	35 [6]	14 [6]	39 [5]	33 [7]	15 [4]	30 [12]	25 [9]	19 [5]	3 [1]	36 [5]
O	29 [5]	18 [8]	31 [4]	5 [1]	15 [4]	5 [2]	17 [6]	15 [4]	40 [12]	7 [1]
P	76 [13]	41 [18]	46 [6]	67 [14]	65 [17]	78 [31]	69 [25]	59 [16]	30 [9]	50 [7]

Tables 5, 6 and 7 show the results of my analysis of the representation of the Greek people within travel writing of the mid-twentieth century. In table 5 the incidence of certain attributes of the Greek people is shown first as a percentage of travel accounts, with the raw number (out of 92) in square brackets. "Positive" indicates where an author agrees with the attachment of this characteristic to the Greeks. "Negative" is where the behaviour described contradicts this representation, or the writer denies the existence of this feature of the Greek character. Thus, for example, 42% of accounts (39 out of 92) describe Greeks (individually or collectively) as brave or heroic; 2% (2 accounts) cite examples of unheroic or cowardly behaviour. In table 6 this information is expressed as the percentage of accounts of each decade (1940s, 1950s, and 1960-74) in which this characteristic is mentioned. Finally, table 7 shows the extent to which authors *consistently* build up a picture of Greeks as friendly, generous, and so on, by listing the percentage of accounts that have *five* or more mentions in each category.

Table 5. The Greeks in travel writing, 1940-74

Characteristic	Positive	Negative
Friendly / curious about others	83 [76]	22 [20]
Generous / hospitable	87 [80]	18 [17]
Attempt to take advantage of travellers	37 [34]	25 [23]
Brave / heroic	42 [39]	2 [2]
Interested in politics / a democratic people	55 [51]	8 [7]
Sociable / garrulous / noisy	78 [72]	38 [35]
Religious / superstitious	66 [61]	18 [17]
Simple or pastoral way of life / timelessness	86 [79]	20 [18]
Images of a classical nature related	66 [61]	5 [5]
Explicit statement about ethnic link to ancient people	29 [27]	24 [22]

Table 6. The Greeks in travel writing, 1940-74 (by decade)

Characteristic	Positive			Negative		
	1940-49	1950-59	1960-74	1940-49	1950-59	1960-74
Friendly / curious about others	70 [7]	90 [26]	81 [43]	20 [2]	38 [11]	13 [7]
Generous / hospitable	80 [8]	90 [26]	87 [46]	10 [1]	31 [9]	13 [7]
Attempt to take advantage of travellers	20 [2]	41 [12]	38 [20]	10 [1]	17 [5]	32 [17]
Brave / heroic	60 [6]	41 [12]	40 [21]	0 [0]	3 [1]	2 [1]
Interested in politics / a democratic people	50 [5]	59 [17]	55 [29]	0 [0]	14 [4]	6 [3]
Sociable / garrulous / noisy	70 [7]	90 [26]	74 [39]	30 [3]	45 [13]	36 [19]
Religious / superstitious	60 [6]	76 [22]	62 [33]	10 [1]	28 [8]	15 [8]
Simple or pastoral way of life / timelessness	80 [8]	90 [26]	85 [45]	10 [1]	38 [11]	11 [6]
Images of a classical nature related	50 [5]	72 [21]	66 [35]	10 [1]	3 [1]	6 [3]
Explicit statement about ethnic link to ancient people	60 [6]	24 [7]	26 [14]	20 [2]	31 [9]	21 [11]

Table 7. Characteristics consistently attributed to the Greek people in travel writing (five or more references in one account)

Characteristic	Positive	Negative
Friendly / curious about others	37 [34]	0 [0]
Generous / hospitable	54 [50]	0 [0]
Attempt to take advantage of travellers	4 [4]	0 [0]
Brave / heroic	2 [2]	0 [0]
Interested in politics / a democratic people	10 [9]	0 [0]
Sociable / garrulous / noisy	35 [32]	2 [2]
Religious / superstitious	33 [30]	0 [0]
Simple or pastoral way of life / timelessness	43 [40]	0 [0]
Images of a classical nature related	12 [11]	0 [0]
Explicit statement about ethnic link to ancient people	1 [1]	0 [0]

Ángel Quintana has warned that "reading meaning into—and coercing meaning out of—texts must be done cautiously" (2001:181). The methodology I have adopted here does not make my conclusions "objective". As Buchignani confessed of his own practices, they are "socially and culturally grounded in larger systems having their own methodological criteria for adequacy and correctness" (2000:147). But at least this approach has allowed me to make assertions about the way Greece is represented in travel literature which are reinforced by a verifiable method and not merely by isolated quotations. It is to be hoped that others will continue to refine the ways in which we establish ideas about representations of the "other" within and across travel texts.

NOTES

[1] The chapters within Eisner (1991) and Cocker (1992) on twentieth century Greek travellers have recently been joined by the work of David Roessel (2003). Roessel views Greece in English and American fiction and travel literature as heavily influenced by Byron: "few countries have remained in the shadow of a single author for so long" (2003:4). Roessel makes useful points about the evolution of travellers' views in the twentieth century, the post-1940 period being the subject of his conclusion (252ff). Henry Miller and Lawrence Durrell receive due attention, and they are also the subject of a recent full-length study by Edmund Keeley (1999).

[2] This seems as good a place as any to point out that, throughout this book, I have attempted to be consistent only in my own usage of Greek place-names and concepts. Where these appear in quotations I have taken from the works of travel writers, historians, and others, I have retained the original spelling. Likewise with passages written in American English.

[3] Shirley Weber's invaluable catalogue of nineteenth century travel books about Greece held by the Gennadius Library was recently reissued (Weber 2002).

[4] The section in Blum and Blum (1970) on continuities from the ancient world is 261ff. Some of the examples given are:

-the system of dowry and marriage (280-1);

-the ceremony for new-born babies, the "pollution" of a new mother, and the fear that the baby could be possessed (271-2);

-demon possession, part of "the psychological apparatus of the Greek culture for many centuries" (309);

-the "evil eye", which has "survived without important changes over several thousands of years" (309-10);

-village medicine, having "more correspondence than difference" (296), including the use of amulets (284, 295);

-many "beliefs related to death and dying . . . are survivals from earlier periods" (314-5), and have simply been overlain by Christianity (321);

-funeral customs, each of which "is found to be a survival of an ancient practice" (314);

-Christ as similar to Asclepius in that he raised the dead, and, in his own resurrection, resembling Dionysus (321);

-nereids, "the nymphs of old", representing a fantasy of how women would like to run wild themselves, as in classical plays by Aristophanes and Euripides (328-9);

-"Stringlos, the dancing half-man, seems a close approximation to Pan or the satyrs" (329);

-hospitality to strangers (296-7).

[5] The actor, novelist and English teacher Kester Berwick (1903-1992) has had an intriguing passage through the literature of residency in Greece. He has most recently appeared as the background presence in Robert Dessaix's novel *Corfu* (2002). Dessaix's characters refer to Betty Roland and her travel book *Lesbos: The Pagan Island* (1963), viewing her as a rather forlorn figure who visited Berwick with romance in mind, not realising that he was more interested in homosexual encounters with local boys (Dessaix 2002:187-90). Having read Roland's book, Joseph Braddock, as we have seen, sought out Berwick during a visit to Lesbos in the mid 1960s (1967:48ff), a meeting of which Dessaix makes no mention. Roland had characterized Berwick's motives in much the same terms as stated in Braddock's later account: "Kester was not worried over small material returns. He was in love with Greece and passionately wanted to remain there" (Roland 1963:23).

[6] Moss' tale of the abduction and evacuation of General Kreipe, published in 1950, was subsequently translated into film by Powell and Pressburger, starring Dirk Bogarde as Patrick Leigh Fermor. By the early 1970s the legend had developed to the extent that Malcolm Napier inaccurately wrote that "Patrick" had "distinguished himself by capturing a German general single-handed" (Napier 1972:69). Thus the incident has, as M. R. D. Foot commented in a recent reissue of Moss' book, come to be "remembered in Great Britain as a tremendous jape" (Moss 2001:9). Other judgements have been less forgiving. In the 1980s another ex-British agent in Crete described this to Roger Jinkinson (2005:68-9) as a "gong hunting expedition" which had led to reprisals: "the *andartes* [resistance fighters] were furious. Their homes and crops were destroyed, their families and friends murdered, for no reason at all." Leigh Fermor has challenged both the adventure and futility interpretations. He maintains that, originally conceived as a "gesture of vengeance" for German actions against civilians, the mission was "a shrewd blow to the German morale and a great lift to ours" (Moss 2001:209). Leigh Fermor's 1969 account, written for the Imperial War Museum, appears in the anthology *Words of Mercury* (2001:88ff).

[7] Reflections on Thermopylae were not restricted to comparisons with the recent behaviour of the Greeks. Ernest Chapman of the 3rd Royal Tank Regiment felt that the rearguard actions of the *British* in mainland Greece had "shades of Leonidas" (Horlington 1991:50). After her 1850 visit to Athens and Corfu, Florence Nightingale wrote a Christian "vision" in which she compared the heroics of Thermopylae to the eternal human struggle against evil (Calabria 1997:142-4).

[8] The reference is to Thucydides, *The Peloponnesian War*, 2.35-46.

[9] The reference is to Thucydides, *The Peloponnesian War*, 1.10. In the translation by Rex Warner, Thucydides writes:

> Suppose, for example, that the city of Sparta were to become deserted and that only the temples and foundations of buildings remained, I think that future generations would, as time passed, find it very difficult to believe that the place had really been as powerful as it was represented to be. (Thucydides 1952:41)

[10] According to Annita Panaretou (2005:120), Greeks travelling in Western Europe during the same period felt no cultural inferiority: "the universality of the achievements of the past made Greek travel writers able to claim an air of equality and, sometimes, superiority." I am not able in this book to analyse the work of Greek travel writers, whether on their own country or elsewhere, as this would require the examination of a number of other discourses. A rare collection of such writings translated into English has been compiled by Artemis Leontis (1997).

[11] See O'Reilly (2000:43-4, 50ff) for a discussion of how the British living in Spain have, similarly, perceived categories amongst migrants.

[12] A fascinating account of a visit to Leigh Fermor at his house in 2002 is included in Robert D. Kaplan's *Mediterranean Winter* (2006:223ff).

[13] Due to further research, this list has been revised from that included in Wills 2005b. The total number of texts is now 92.

[14] The number of texts published in each decade is as follows: 10 (1940-49), 29 (1950-59), and 53 (1960-74).

BIBLIOGRAPHY

Adams, Phoebe-Lou. 1965. *A Rough Map of Greece*. London: Hutchinson.

Alexander, G. M. 1982. *The Prelude to the Truman Doctrine: British Policy in Greece, 1944-47*. Oxford: Oxford University Press.

Alexander, Guy. 7 August 2004. "An Olympian Feat: How Athens Defied Critics and Got Ready in Time for the Games." *Independent*, 3.

Andersen, Hans Christian. 1842. *A Poet's Bazaar: A Journey to Greece, Turkey and up the Danube*. Reprint, translated by Grace Thornton, New York: Michael Kesend, 1988.

Anderson, Patrick. 1958. *First Steps in Greece*. London: Chatto and Windus.

—. 1963. *Dolphin Days: A Writer's Notebook on Mediterranean Pleasures*. London: Gollancz.

—. 1964. *The Smile of Apollo: A Literary Companion to Greek Travel*. London: Chatto and Windus.

Andrews, Kevin. 1959. *The Flight of Ikaros: A Journey into Greece*. London: Weidenfeld and Nicolson.

—. 1979. *Athens Alive*. Athens: Hermes.

Angelomatis-Tsougarakis, Helen. 1990. *The Eve of the Greek Revival: British Travellers' Perceptions of Early Nineteenth-Century Greece*. London: Routledge.

Arnold, Sue. 20 May 2006. Review of *Bitter Lemons of Cyprus*, by Lawrence Durrell (audiobook). *Guardian*, Review section, 18.

Balfour, Patrick. 1951. *The Orphaned Realm: Journeys in Cyprus*. London: Percival Marshall.

Barber, Giles. 1999. "The English-Language Guide Book to Europe up to 1870." In *Journeys Through the Market: Travel, Travellers and the Book Trade*, ed. Robin Myers and Michael Harris, 93-106. Kent and New Castle, DE: St Paul's Bibliographies and Oak Knoll Press.

Barber, Robin. 2002. *Blue Guide: Athens*. London: A & C Black.

Barrell, John. 1991. "Death on the Nile: Fantasy and the Literature of Tourism, 1850-60." *Essays in Criticism* 41:97-127.

Barthes, Roland. 1979. *The Eiffel Tower, and Other Mythologies*. Translated by Richard Howard. New York: Hill and Wang.

Bassnett, Susan. 1999. "Interview with Colin Thubron." *Studies in Travel Writing* 3:148-71.

—. 2002. "Travel Writing and Gender." In *The Cambridge Companion to Travel Writing*, ed. Peter Hulme and Tim Youngs, 225-41. Cambridge: Cambridge University Press.

Beard, Mary. 2002. *The Parthenon*. London: Profile.

Beard, Mary, and John Henderson. 1995. *Classics: A Very Short Introduction*. Oxford: Oxford University Press.

Beevor, Anthony. 1992. *Crete: The Battle and the Resistance*. London: Penguin.

Bell, Robert. 1961. *By Road to Greece*. London: Alvin Redman.

Bent, J. Theodore. 1885. *The Cyclades*. Reprint, Oxford: Archaeopress, 2002.

Billig, Michael. 1995. *Banal Nationalism*. London: Sage.

Birand, M. A. 1985. *30 Hot Days*. Nicosia: K. Rustem.

Black, Jeremy. 2003. *Italy and the Grand Tour*. New Haven: Yale University Press.

Blum, Richard, and Eva Blum. 1970. *The Dangerous Hour: The Lore and Culture of Crisis and Mystery in Rural Greece*. London: Chatto and Windus.

Blunt, Alison. 1994. *Travel, Gender and Imperialism: Mary Kingsley and West Africa*. New York: Guilford Press.

Bowman, Glenn. 2000. "Christian Ideology and the Image of a Holy Land." In *Contesting the Sacred: The Anthropology of Pilgrimage*, ed. John Eade and Michael J. Sallnow, 98-121. London: Routledge.

Braddock, Joseph. 1967. *Some Greek Islands: The Shores of Light*. London: Robert Hale.

—. 1970. *Sappho's Island: A Paean for Lesbos*. London: Constable.

Bray, Roger, and Vladimir Raitz. 2001. *Flight to the Sun: The Story of the Holiday Revolution*. London: Continuum.

Breay, Claire. 1999. "Women and the Classical Tripos 1869-1914." In *Classics in 19th and 20th Century Cambridge: Curriculum, Culture and Community*, ed. Christopher Stray, 49-70. Cambridge: Cambridge Philological Society, supplementary vol. 24.

Brockway, Lucile, and George Brockway. 1966. *Greece: A Classical Tour with Extras*. London: Gollancz.

Brook, Ian. 1971. *A Sea Blue Boat, and a Sun God's Island*. London: Adland Coles.

Brothers, A. J. 1997. "Travellers to Greece and the Levant in the Seventeenth and Eighteenth Centuries." In *The Founders' Library, University of Wales, Lampeter: Bibliographical and Contextual Studies*, ed. W. Marx, *Trivium* 29/30:99-124.

Brown, K. S. and Yannis Hamilakis, eds. 2003. *The Usable Past: Greek Metahistories*. Lanham: Lexington.

Buchignani, Norman. 2000. "Idleness in South Africa Re-visited: Ethnographic Methods and 'Hottentot' Travel Accounts." *Journeys: The International Journal of Travel and Travel Writing* 1:114-56.

Bull, Peter. 1967. *It Isn't All Greek to Me*. London: Peter Davies.

Bulwer, John. 2006. "United Kingdom." In *Classics Teaching in Europe*, ed. John Bulwer, 124-31. London: Duckworth.

Burnell, F. S. 1931. *Wanderings in Greece*. London: Edward Arnold.

Byron, Robert. 1928. *The Station: Athos; Treasures and Men*. Reprint, London: Phoenix Press, 2000.

Calabria, Michael D. 1997. *Florence Nightingale in Greece and Egypt: Her Diary and "Visions"*. Albany: State University of New York Press.

Cambridge, Diana, ed. 2006. *Buying a Property in Greece and the Islands*. Bath: Merricks Media.

Campbell, J. K. 1964. *Honour, Family, and Patronage: A Study of Institutions and Moral Values in a Greek Mountain Community*. Oxford: Oxford University Press.

—. 1992. "Fieldwork among the Sarakatsani, 1954-55." In *Europe Observed*, ed. João de Pina-Cabral and John Campbell, 148-66. London: Macmillan.

Carroll, Michael. 1965. *Gates of the Wind*. London: John Murray.

Casson, Stanley. 1943. *Greece and Britain*. London: Collins.

Chamberlain, Brenda. 1965. *A Rope of Vines: Journal from a Greek Island*. London: Hodder and Stoughton.

Chapman, Olive Murray. 1937. *Across Cyprus*. London: The Bodley Head.

Chard, Chloe. 1999. *Pleasure and Guilt on the Grand Tour: Travel Writing and Imaginative Geography 1600-1830*. Manchester: Manchester University Press.

Chatto, James. 2005. *The Greek for Love*. London: John Murray.

Clark, Alan. 2000. *The Fall of Crete*. London: Cassell.

Clift, Charmian. 1958. *Mermaid Singing*. London: Michael Joseph.

—. 1959. *Peel me a Lotus*. London: Hutchinson.

Close, David H. 2002. *Greece Since 1945*. London: Longman.

Cocker, Mark. 1992. *Loneliness and Time: British Travel Writing in the Twentieth Century*. London: Secker and Warburg.

Coles, S. F. A. 1965. *Greece: A Journey in Time*. London: Robert Hale.

Constantine, David. 1984. *Early Greek Travellers and the Hellenic Ideal*. Cambridge: Cambridge University Press.

Cook, Sylvia, and Terry Cook, eds. 2002. *The Greek-o-File* vol. 1.
—. 2003. *The Greek-o-File* vol. 2.
—. 2006. *The Greek-o-File* vol. 5.
Craik, Jennifer. 1997. "The Culture of Tourism." In *Touring Cultures: Transformations of Travel and Theory*, ed. Chris Rojek and John Urry, 113-36. London: Routledge.
Crawshaw, Carol, and John Urry. 1997. "Tourism and the Photographic Eye." In *Touring Cultures: Transformations of Travel and Theory*, ed. Chris Rojek and John Urry, 176-95. London: Routledge.
Crick, Malcolm. 1995. "The Anthropologist as Tourist: An Identity in Question." In *International Tourism*, ed. M.-F. Lanfant, J. B. Allcock, and E. M. Bruner, 205-23. London: Sage.
Crook, J. Mordaunt. 1972. *The Greek Revival: Neo-Classical Attitudes in British Architecture 1760-1870*. Rev. ed. London: John Murray, 1995.
Curtis, William J. R. 1997. *Modern Architecture, Mythical Landscapes and Ancient Ruins*. London: Sir John Soane's Museum.
Damer, G. L. Dawson. 1842. *Diary of a Tour in Greece, Turkey, Egypt and the Holy Land*. Vol. 1. London: Henry Colburn.
Davies, Norman. 1997. *Europe: A History*. London: Pimlico.
Davis, J. 1977. *People of the Mediterranean*. London: Routledge and Kegan Paul.
Dessaix, Robert. 2002. *Corfu: A Novel*. London: Scribner.
Dodge, David. 1955. *Talking Turkey*. London: Arthur Barker.
du Boulay, Juliet. 1974. *Portrait of a Greek Mountain Village*. Oxford: Oxford University Press.
—. 1991. "Strangers and Gifts: Hostility and Hospitality in Rural Greece." *Journal of Mediterranean Studies* 1:37-53.
Durrell, Gerald. 1959. *My Family and Other Animals*. Harmondsworth: Penguin.
—. 1978. *The Garden of the Gods*. London: Collins.
—. 2006. *The Corfu Trilogy*. London: Penguin.
Durrell, Lawrence. 1945. *Prospero's Cell*. London: Faber.
—. 1953. *Reflections on a Marine Venus: A Companion to the Landscape of Rhodes*. London: Faber.
—. 1957. *Bitter Lemons of Cyprus*. London: Faber.
—. 1969. *Spirit of Place*. Edited by Alan G. Thomas. London: Faber.
Duxbury, Ken. 1973. *Lugworm on the Loose: Exploring Greece in an Open Dinghy*. London: Pelham.
Eisner, Robert. 1991. *Travelers to an Antique Land: The History and Literature of Travel to Greece*. Ann Arbor: University of Michigan Press.

Eliot, Alexander. 1964. *Greece*. Netherlands: Time-Life International.

Enfield, Edward. 2003. *Greece on my Wheels*. Chichester: Summersdale.

Ervine, St. John. 1936. *A Journey to Jerusalem*. London: Hamish Hamilton.

Evans, Stanley. 1965. *In Evening Dress to Calvary: A Few Days in Palestine and Greece*. London: S. C. M.

Ferguson, Hugh. 2001. "William Martin Leake and the Greek Revival." In *Travellers in the Levant: Voyagers and Visionaries*, ed. Sarah Seawright and Malcolm Wagstaff, 17-34. Durham: ASTENE.

Ferris, David S. 2000. *Silent Urns: Romanticism, Hellenism, Modernity*. Stanford: Stanford University Press.

Fielding, Xan. 1953. *The Stronghold: An Account of the Four Seasons in the White Mountains of Crete*. London: Secker and Warburg.

Finer, Leslie. 1964. *Passport to Greece*. London: Longmans.

Fitton, J. Lesley. 1995. *The Discovery of the Greek Bronze Age*. London: British Museum.

Fleming, K. E. 2000. "*Orientalism*, the Balkans, and Balkan Historiography." *American Historical Review* 105:1218-33.

Forbes, Duncan. 1970. *The Heart of Greece*. London: Robert Hale.

Forbes-Boyd, Eric. 1965. *In Crusader Greece*. London: Centaur.

—. 1970. *Aegean Quest: A Search for Venetian Greece*. London: Dent.

Forrest, Martin. 1996. *Modernising the Classics: A Study in Curriculum Development*. Exeter: University of Exeter.

Forte, John Knox, ed. 1964. *Corfu: Venus of the Isles*. East Essex Gazette.

Foss, Arthur. 1969. *The Ionian Islands*. London: Faber.

Frawley, Maria H. 1994. *A Wider Range: Travel Writing by Women in Victorian England*. London: Associated University Presses.

Freeman, Edward A. 1893. *Studies of Travel: Greece*. London: Putnam.

Friedl, Ernestine. 1962. *Vasilika: A Village in Modern Greece*. New York: Holt, Rinehart and Winston.

—. 1970. "Fieldwork in a Greek Village." In *Women in the Field: Anthropological Experiences*, ed. Peggy Golde, 195-217. Berkeley: University of California Press.

Friedman, Jonathan. 1992. "The Past in the Future: History and the Politics of Identity." *American Anthropologist* 94:837-59.

Gage, Eleni. 2004. *North of Ithaka*. London: Bantam.

Gage, Nicholas. 1983. *Eleni*. London: Collins Harvill.

Galani-Moutafi, Vasiliki. 2000. "The Self and the Other: Traveler, Ethnographer, Tourist." *Annals of Tourism Research* 27:203-24.

Garnett, David. 1942. *The Campaign in Greece and Crete*. London: H. M. S. O.

Garrett, Martin. 1994. *Greece: A Literary Companion*. London: John Murray.

Gere, Cathy. 2006. *The Tomb of Agamemnon*. London: Profile.

Gibbons, Jean D. and Mary Fish. 1990. "Greece: Update on the Gods and Holidays." *Annals of Tourism Research* 17:473-5.

Gifford, Eric. 1939. *East of Athens*. London: The Travel Book Club.

Golding, Louis. 1955. *Goodbye to Ithaca*. London: Hutchinson.

Gould Lee, Arthur S. 1948. *The Royal House of Greece*. London: Ward Lock.

Greenhalgh, Peter, and Edward Eliopoulos. 1985. *Deep Into Mani*. London: Faber.

Greece. July/August 2004. Issue 7.

Hadjipateras, C. N. and M. S. Fafalios. 1995. *Greece 1940-41 Eyewitnessed*. Anixi: Efstathiadis.

Hall, Edith. 1999. "Medea and British Legislation before the First World War." *Greece and Rome*, 2nd ser., 46:42-77.

Hamilakis, Yannis, and Eleana Yalouri. 1996. "Antiquities as Symbolic Capital in Modern Greek Society." *Antiquity* 70(267):117-29.

Hardwick, Lorna. 2003. *Reception Studies. Greece and Rome* New Surveys in the Classics 33. Oxford: Oxford University Press.

Herzfeld, Michael. 1987. *Anthropology Through the Looking-Glass: Critical Ethnography in the Margins of Europe*. Cambridge: Cambridge University Press.

Hill Miller, Helen. 1962. *Greek Horizons*. London: George G. Harrap.

—. 1972. *Greece Through the Ages: As Seen by Travellers from Herodotus to Byron*. London: Dent.

Hirschon, Renée. 1989. *Heirs of the Greek Catastrophe: The Social Life of Asia Minor Refugees in Piraeus*. Reprint, Oxford: Berghahn, 1998.

Hitchens, Christopher. 1997. *Hostage to History: Cyprus from the Ottomans to Kissinger*. London: Verso.

Hobsbawm, E. J. 1992. *Nations and Nationalism Since 1780*. Cambridge: Cambridge University Press.

Hogarth, Paul. 1953. *Defiant People*. London: Lawrence and Wishart.

Holland, Robert, and Diana Markides. 2006. *The British and the Hellenes: Struggles for Mastery in the Eastern Mediterranean 1850-1960*. Oxford: Oxford University Press.

Hooker, G. T. W. ed. 1963. *Parthenos and Parthenon. Greece and Rome* supplement to volume X. Oxford: Oxford University Press.

Horlington, Edwin, ed. 1991. *Tell Them We Were Here: 1940-1941 Greek Campaign*. Walton on the Naze: Edlington Press.

Hounsell, Roy. 2007. *The Papas and the Englishman: From Corfu to Zagoria*. Twickenham: Yiannis Books.

Hughes, Glyn. 1976. *Fair Prospects: Journeys in Greece*. London: Gollancz.

Hughes, Hilda, ed. 1944. *The Glory that is Greece*. London: Hutchinson.

Hugo, Howard E. ed. 1977. *The Portable Romantic Reader*. Harmondsworth: Penguin.

Hulme, Peter, and Tim Youngs, eds. 2002. *The Cambridge Companion to Travel Writing*. Cambridge: Cambridge University Press.

Hunter, Isobel L. 1947. *This is Greece*. London: Evans Brothers.

Hutton, Edward. 1928. *A Glimpse of Greece*. London: The Medici Society.

Huxley, Davina. 2001. "Leake in Kythera." In *Travellers in the Levant: Voyagers and Visionaries*, ed. Sarah Seawright and Malcolm Wagstaff, 35-41. Durham: ASTENE.

Jenkins, Romilly. 1961. *The Dilessi Murders: Greek Brigands and English Hostages*. Reprint, London: Prion, 1998.

Jenkyns, Richard. 1980. *The Victorians and Ancient Greece*. Oxford: Blackwell.

—. 1991. *Dignity and Decadence: Victorian Art and the Classical Inheritance*. London: Harper Collins.

Jinkinson, Roger, 2005. *Tales from a Greek Island*. London: The Racing House Press.

John, Evan. 1954. *Time after Earthquake: An Adventure Among Greek Islands in August, 1953*. London: Heinemann.

Jones, Stephen, Christopher Newall, Leonée Ormond, Richard Ormond, and Benedict Read. 1996. *Frederic Leighton*. London: Royal Academy of Arts.

Just, Roger. 2000. *A Greek Island Cosmos: Kinship and Community on Meganisi*. Santa Fe and Oxford: SAR / Currey.

Kanelli, Sheelagh. 1965. *Earth and Water: A Marriage into Greece*. London: Hodder and Stoughton.

Kaplan, Caren. 1996. *Questions of Travel: Postmodern Discourses of Displacement*. Durham, North Carolina: Duke University Press.

Kaplan, Robert D. 2006. *Mediterranean Winter: A Journey Through History*. London: Arrow.

Kark, Austen. 1994. *Attic in Greece*. London: Little, Brown.

Keeley, Edmund. 1999. *Inventing Paradise: The Greek Journey 1937-47*. New York: Farrar, Straus and Giroux.

Kenna, Margaret E. 1992. "Changing Places and Altered Perspectives: Research on a Greek Island in the 1960s and in the 1980s." In

Anthropology and Autobiography, ed. Judith Okely and Helen Callaway, 147-62. London: Routledge.

Kimbrough, Emily. 1957. *Water, Water Everywhere*. London: Heinemann.

——. 1965. *Forever Old, Forever New*. London: Heinemann.

Kininmonth, Christopher. 1949. *The Children of Thetis: A Study of Islands and Islanders in the Aegean*. London: John Lehmann.

Kizilos, Katherine. 1997. *The Olive Grove*. Melbourne: Lonely Planet.

Knowles, John. 1964. *Double Vision: American Thoughts Abroad*. London: Secker and Warburg.

Krippner, Monica. 1957. *Beyond Athens: Journeys Through Greece*. London: Geoffrey Bles.

Kubly, Herbert. 1970. *Gods and Heroes*. London: Gollancz.

Lancaster, Osbert. 1947. *Classical Landscape with Figures*. London: John Murray.

Larson, Victoria Tietze. 1999. "Classics and the Acquisition and Validation of Power in Britain's 'Imperial Century' (1815-1914)." *International Journal of the Classical Tradition* 6(2):185-225.

Lawrence, Karen. 1994. *Penelope Voyages: Women and Travel in the British Literary Tradition*. Ithaca: Cornell University Press.

Lee, C. P. 1957. *Athenian Adventure: With Alarums and Excursions*. London: Gollancz.

Lee, Laurie, and Ralph Keene. 1947. *We Made a Film in Cyprus*. London: Longmans.

Leeper, Reginald. 1950. *When Greek Meets Greek*. London: Chatto and Windus.

Leigh Fermor, Patrick. 1958. *Mani: Travels in the Southern Peloponnese*. Reprint, Harmondsworth: Penguin, 1984.

——. 1966. *Roumeli: Travels in Northern Greece*. London: John Murray.

——. 2003. *Words of Mercury*. Edited by Artemis Cooper. London: John Murray.

Leontis, Artemis, ed. 1997. *Greece: A Traveler's Literary Companion*. San Francisco: Whereabouts Press.

Levy, H. L. 1956. "Property Distribution by Lot in Present Day Greece." *Transactions of the American Philological Association* 87:42-6.

Liddell, Robert. 1954. *Aegean Greece*. London: Jonathan Cape.

——. 1958. *The Morea*. London: Jonathan Cape.

——. 1965. *Mainland Greece*. London: Longmans.

Livingstone, R. W. 1916. *A Defence of Classical Education*. London: Macmillan.

——., ed. 1923. *The Pageant of Greece*. Oxford: Oxford University Press.

Loch, Joice NanKivell. 1968. *A Fringe of Blue*. London: John Murray.

Lowenthal, David. 1985. *The Past is a Foreign Country*. Cambridge: Cambridge University Press.

Luke, Harry. 1965. *Cyprus: A Portrait and an Appreciation*. London: George G. Harrap.

MacCannell, Dean. 1976. *The Tourist: A New Theory of the Leisure Class*. London: Macmillan.

MacDonald, Callum. 1995. *The Lost Battle: Crete, 1941*. London: Papermac.

MacGillivray, J. Alexander. 2001. *Minotaur: Sir Arthur Evans and the Archaeology of the Minoan Myth*. London: Pimlico.

Macgregor Morris, Ian. 2000. "'To Make a New Thermopylae': Hellenism, Greek Liberation and the Battle of Thermopylae." *Greece and Rome*, 2nd ser., 47:211-30.

MacKendrick, Paul. 1962. *The Greek Stones Speak: The Story of Archaeology in Greek Lands*. London: Methuen.

Mackenzie, Compton. 1960. *Greece in My Life*. London: Chatto and Windus.

MacLean, Rory. 2004. *Falling for Icarus*. London: Viking.

MacNiven, Ian. 1998. *Lawrence Durrell: A Biography*. London: Faber.

Macvicar, Neil. 1990. *A Heart's Odyssey*. Salisbury: Michael Russell.

Mais, S. P. B. and Gillian Mais. 1962. *Greek Holiday*. London: Alvin Redman.

Marchand, Suzanne L. 1996. *Down from Olympus: Archaeology and Philhellenism in Germany, 1750-1970*. Princeton: Princeton University Press.

Martindale, Charles, and Richard F. Thomas, eds. 2006. *Classics and the Uses of Reception*. Blackwell: Oxford.

Matthews, Carola. 1968. *The Mad Pomegranate Tree: An Image of Modern Greece*. London: Macmillan.

—. 1971. *At the Top of the Muletrack*. London: Macmillan.

Mauzy, Craig A. 2006. *Agora Excavations 1931-2006: A Pictorial History*. Athens: The American School of Classical Studies at Athens.

Mazower, Mark. 2000. *The Balkans*. London: Weidenfeld and Nicolson.

—. 2001. *Inside Hitler's Greece: The Experience of Occupation, 1941-44*. New Haven: Yale University Press.

McKevitt, Christopher. 2000. "San Giovanni Rotondo and the Shrine of Padre Pio." In *Contesting the Sacred: The Anthropology of Pilgrimage*, ed. John Eade and Michael J. Sallnow, 76-97. London: Routledge.

Meethan, Kevin. 2001. *Tourism in Global Society: Place, Culture, Consumption*. Basingstoke: Palgrave.

Merrill, Christopher. 2004. *Journey to the Holy Mountain: Meditations on Mount Athos*. London: Harper Collins.

Middleton, Robin. 2004. Introd. to *The Ruins of the Most Beautiful Monuments of Greece*, by Julien-David Le Roy. Los Angeles: Getty.

Mikes, George. 1965. *Eureka! Rummaging in Greece*. London: Andre Deutsch.

Miller, Henry. 1942. *The Colossus of Maroussi*. Reprint, London: Minerva, 1991.

Miller, William. 1905. *Greek Life in Town and Country*. London: George Newnes.

Mills, Sara. 1991. *Discourses of Difference: An Analysis of Women's Travel Writing and Colonialism*. London: Routledge.

Ministry of Reconstruction. 1919. *The Classics in British Education*. Reconstruction Problems 21. London: Ministry of Reconstruction.

Minta, Stephen. 1998. *On a Voiceless Shore: Byron in Greece*. New York: Henry Holt.

Mole, John. 2004. *It's All Greek to Me!* London: Nicholas Brealey.

Morpurgo, J. E. 1963. *The Road to Athens*. London: Eyre and Spottiswoode.

Morris, Jan, ed. 1993. *Travels with Virginia Woolf*. London: Hogarth Press.

Morton, H. V. 1936. *In the Steps of St. Paul*. London: Rich and Cowan.

—. 1941. *Middle East*. London: Methuen.

Moss, W. Stanley. 2001. *Ill Met by Moonlight*. London: The Folio Society.

Mustoe, Anne. 2003. *Cleopatra's Needle*. London: Virgin Books.

Myers, E. C. W. 1985. *Greek Entanglement*. Gloucester: Alan Sutton.

Napier, Malcolm. 1972. *An Anthology*. London: Regency Press.

Nisbet, Gideon. 2006. *Ancient Greece in Film and Popular Culture*. Exeter: Bristol Phoenix Press.

Noel-Baker, Francis. 1967. *Looking at Greece*. London: Black / Lippincott.

O'Malley, Brendan, and Ian Craig. 1999. *The Cyprus Conspiracy: America, Espionage and the Turkish Invasion*. London: I. B. Tauris.

O'Reilly, Karen. 2000. *The British on the Costa del Sol*. London: Routledge.

Osler, Michael. 1957. *Journey to Hattusas*. London: Hutchinson.

Ouditt, Sharon. 2006. "'Elemental and Permanent Things': George Gissing and Norman Douglas in Southern Italy." *Studies in Travel Writing* 10:123-40.

Panaretou, Annita. 2005. "Particularities of Greek Travel Writing in a Balkan and European Context." *Journeys: The International Journal of Travel and Travel Writing* 6:117-22.

Patmore, Derek. 1944. *Images of Greece*. London: Country Life.

Payne, Robert. 1961. *The Splendour of Greece*. London: Robert Hale.

—. 1965. *The Isles of Greece*. London: Hamish Hamilton.

Pearce, Philip L. 2005. *Tourist Behaviour: Themes and Conceptual Schemes*. Clevedon: Channel View Publications.

Peckham, Robert Shannon. 1999. "The Exoticism of the Familiar and the Familiarity of the Exotic: *Fin-de-siecle* Travellers to Greece." In *Writes of Passage: Reading Travel Writing*, ed. James Duncan and Derek Gregory, 164-84. London: Routledge.

—. 2001. *National Histories, Natural States: Nationalism and the Politics of Place in Greece*. London: I. B. Tauris.

Pemble, John. 1987. *The Mediterranean Passion: Victorians and Edwardians in the South*. Oxford: Oxford University Press.

Pentreath, Guy. 1964. *Hellenic Traveller: A Guide to the Ancient Sites of Greece and the Aegean*. London: Faber.

Plouviez, Charles. 2001. "Straddling the Aegean: William Gell 1811-1813." In *Travellers in the Levant: Voyagers and Visionaries*, ed. Sarah Seawright and Malcolm Wagstaff, 42-56. Durham: ASTENE.

Pollard, John. 1955. *Journey to the Styx*. London: Christopher Johnson.

Ponder, John. 1997. *Patriots and Scoundrels: Behind Enemy Lines in Wartime Greece, 1943-44*. Melbourne: Hyland House.

Pouqueville, F. C. H. L. 1820. *Travels in Epirus, Albania, Macedonia and Thessaly*. Reprint, ed. James Pettifer, Classic Balkan Travel Series, n.d.

Powell, Dilys. 1941. *Remember Greece*. London: Hodder and Stoughton.

—. 1943. *The Traveller's Journey is Done*. London: Hodder and Stoughton.

—. 1957. *An Affair of the Heart*. London: Hodder and Stoughton.

—. 1973. *The Villa Ariadne*. London: Hodder and Stoughton.

Pratt, Mary Louise. 1992. *Imperial Eyes: Travel Writing and Transculturalism*. London: Routledge.

Psychoundakis, George. 1955. *The Cretan Runner: His Story of the German Occupation*. Translated by Patrick Leigh Fermor. Reprint, London: Penguin, 1998.

Quintana, Ángel Gurría. 2001. "Travelling Through Discourse, Discoursing on Travel: Recent Writing on Travel Literature and British Travellers in Mexico." *Studies in Travel Writing* 5:172-88.

Ragan, John David. 2001. "French Women Travellers in Egypt: A
    Discourse Marginal to Orientalism?" In *Travellers in Egypt*, ed. Paul
    Starkey and Janet Starkey, 222-30. London: Tauris Parke.
Rawson, Elizabeth. 1969. *The Spartan Tradition in European Thought*.
    Oxford: Oxford University Press.
Renan, Ernest. 1882. "What is a Nation?" Reprint, *Nation and Narration*,
    translated and annotated by Martin Thom, ed. Homi K. Bhabha, 8-22.
    London: Routledge, 1990.
Rickard, Ann. 2004. *Not Another Greek Salad*. Sydney: New Holland.
Robertson, Jean, and Duncan Gardiner. 1972. *Twelve Days in Crete*.
    London: Times Newspapers.
Rodenwaldt, Gerhart. 1930. *The Acropolis*, 2nd ed. Oxford: Basil
    Blackwell, 1957.
Roessel, David. 2003. *In Byron's Shadow: Modern Greece in the English
    and American Imagination*. Oxford: Oxford University Press.
Rojek, Chris. 1997. "Indexing, Dragging and the Social Construction of
    Tourist Sights." In *Touring Cultures: Transformations of Travel and
    Theory*, ed. Chris Rojek and John Urry, 52-74. London: Routledge.
Roland, Betty. 1963. *Lesbos: The Pagan Island*. London: Angus and
    Robertson.
Ross, John F. L. 1999. *It's All Greece to Me*. Athens: Athens News.
Rowan-Robinson, H. [1942?] *Wavell in the Middle East*. London:
    Hutchinson.
Rowland, Lyn [Elias Yialouris]. 2000. *The Survival of "Titch" in Hitler's
    Greece*. Athens: Efstathiadis.
Russell, Willy. 1988. *Shirley Valentine*. London: Methuen.
Said, Edward W. 1985. *Orientalism*. Harmondsworth: Peregrine.
Sarrinikolaou, George. 2004. *Facing Athens: Encounters with the Modern
    City*. New York: North Point Press.
Saunders, Michael. 2005. *Everyday Life in the Village*. Athens: Athens
    News.
Schiffer, Reinhold. 2001. "Agatha's Arabs: Agatha Christie in the
    Tradition of British Oriental Travellers." In *Agatha Christie and
    Archaeology*, ed. Charlotte Trumpler, 303-33. London: British
    Museum.
Schildt, Goran. 1953. *In the Wake of Odysseus*. Translated from the
    Swedish by Alan Blair. London: Staples.
Severin, Tim. 1985. *The Jason Voyage: The Quest for the Golden Fleece*.
    London: Hutchinson.
Severis, Rita C. 2000. *Travelling Artists in Cyprus 1700-1960*. London:
    Philip Wilson.

Shanks, Michael. 1996. *The Classical Archaeology of Greece: Experiences of the Discipline*. London: Routledge.

Shields, Rodney. 2005. *Margarita's Olive Press*. London: Ziji.

Sillitoe, Alan. 1996. *Leading the Blind: A Century of Guidebook Travel 1815-1911*. London: Papermac.

Simpson, Colin. 1969. *Greece: The Unclouded Eye*. London: Hodder and Stoughton.

Smith, Anthony D. 1986. *The Ethnic Origins of Nations*. Oxford: Blackwell.

Smith, Ashley. 1948. *Greece: Moments of Grace*. London: Eyre and Spottiswood.

Smith, Michael Llewellyn. 1965. *The Great Island: A Study of Crete*. London: Longmans.

Smyth, Ethel. 1927. *A Three-Legged Tour in Greece*. London: Heinemann.

Spain, Nancy. 1964. *A Funny Thing Happened on the Way*. London: Hutchinson.

Spencer, Matthew. 2000. *Athos: Travels on the Holy Mountain*. London: Azure.

Spencer, Terence. 1954. *Fair Greece, Sad Relic: Literary Philhellenism from Shakespeare to Byron*. Reprint, Bath: Chivers, 1974.

Spratt, T. A. B. 1865. *Travels and Researches in Crete*. Vol. 1. London: John Van Voorst.

St. Clair, William. 1998. *Lord Elgin and the Marbles*. Oxford: Oxford University Press.

Stark, Freya. 1956. *The Lycian Shore: Along the Coast of Turkey by Yacht*. Reprint, London: Century, 1989.

Stefanidis, Ioannis D. 1999. *Isle of Discord: Nationalism, Imperialism and the Making of the Cyprus Problem*. London: Hurst.

Stobart, J. C. 1911. *The Glory that was Greece: A Survey of Hellenic Culture and Civilisation*. Rev. 2nd ed. London: Sidgwick and Jackson, 1915.

Stoneman, Richard. 1984. *A Literary Companion to Travel in Greece*. London: Penguin.

Storace, Patricia. 1997. *Dinner With Persephone: Travels in Greece*. London: Granta.

Stray, Christopher. 1992. *The Living Word: W. H. D. Rouse and the Crisis of Classics in Edwardian England*. London: Duckworth.

—. 1998. *Classics Transformed: Schools, Universities, and Society in England, 1830-1960*. Oxford: Oxford University Press.

—., ed. 1999. *Classics in 19th and 20th Century Cambridge: Curriculum, Culture and Community.* Cambridge: Cambridge Philological Society, supplementary vol. 24.

—., ed. 2006. *Travellers to Greece.* London: The Classical Association.

Summerson, John. 1964. *The Classical Language of Architecture.* London: Methuen.

Sykes, John. 1965. *Caïque: A Portrait of Greek Islanders.* London: Hutchinson.

Taplin, Oliver. 1989. *Greek Fire.* London: Jonathan Cape.

Tennant, Emma. 2002. *A House in Corfu.* London: Vintage.

Thucydides. 1952. *The Peloponnesian War.* Translated by Rex Warner. Rev. ed. Harmondsworth: Penguin, 1972.

Thurston, Hazel. 1960. *From Darkest Mum.* London: Chapman and Hall.

Times. 6 December 2002. "Dialing Wolf", 17.

Todorova, Maria. 1994. "The Balkans: From Discovery to Invention." *Slavic Review* 53:453-82.

Tomkinson, John L. ed. 2002. *Travellers' Greece: Memories of an Enchanted Land.* Athens: Anagnosis.

Toulmin, Stephen. 1963. *Night Sky at Rhodes.* London: Methuen.

Tournikiotis, Panayotis, ed. 1996. *The Parthenon and Its Impact in Modern Times.* Athens: Melissa Publishing House / Harry Abrams.

Toy, Barbara. 1970. *Rendezvous in Cyprus.* London: John Murray.

Tozer, Henry Fanshawe. 1890. *The Islands of the Aegean.* Oxford: Oxford University Press.

Traill, David A. 1995. *Schliemann of Troy: Treasure and Deceit.* New York: St. Martin's Press.

Travis, William. 1970. *Bus Stop Symi.* London: Rapp and Whiting.

Travlou, Penny. 2002. "Go Athens: A Journey to the Centre of the City." In *Tourism: Between Place and Performance*, ed. Simon Coleman and Mike Crang, 108-27. Oxford: Berghahn.

Tremayne, Penelope. 1958. *Below the Tide.* London: Hutchinson.

Tsigakou, Fani-Maria. 1981. *The Rediscovery of Greece: Travellers and Painters of the Romantic Era.* London: Thames and Hudson.

—. 1991. *Through Romantic Eyes: European Images of Nineteenth-Century Greece from the Benaki Museum, Athens.* Alexandria, Virginia: Art Services International.

Turner, Frank. 1981. *The Greek Heritage in Victorian Britain.* New Haven: Yale University Press.

—. 1989. "Why the Greeks and not the Romans in Victorian Britain?" In *Rediscovering Hellenism: The Hellenic Inheritance and the English*

Imagination, ed. G. W. Clarke, 61-81. Cambridge: Cambridge University Press.

Turner, Katherine S. H. 1999. "From Classical to Imperial: Changing Visions of Turkey in the Eighteenth Century." In *Travel Writing and Empire: Postcolonial Theory in Transit*, ed. Steve Clark, 113-28. London: Zed.

Urry, John. 1990. *The Tourist Gaze*. London: Sage.

—. 1995. *Consuming Places*. London: Routledge.

Vermeulen, Hans. 1983. "Urban Research in Greece." In *Urban Life in Mediterranean Europe: Anthropological Perspectives*, ed. Michael Kenny and David I. Kertzer, 109-32. Urbana: University of Illinois Press.

Vrettos, Theodore. 1997. *The Elgin Affair: The Abduction of Antiquity's Greatest Treasures and the Passions it Aroused*. New York: Arcade.

Vyvyan, C. C. 1955. *Temples and Flowers: A Journey to Greece*. London: Peter Owen.

Wagstaff, Malcolm. 2004. *The Contribution of Early Travel Narratives to the Historical Geography of Greece (The 22nd J. L. Myres Memorial Lecture)*. Oxford: University of Oxford.

Waller, John. 2004. *Greek Walls: An Odyssey in Corfu*. Twickenham: Yiannis Books.

—. 2005. *Corfu Sunset: Avrio Never Comes*. Twickenham: Yiannis Books.

Warner, Rex. 1950. *Views of Attica and its Surroundings*. London: John Lehmann.

Watkin, David, and Rhodri Windsor Liscombe. 2000. *The Age of Wilkins: The Architecture of Improvement*. Cambridge: Downing College.

Waugh, Evelyn. 1930. *Labels: A Mediterranean Journal*. London: Duckworth.

Weber, Shirley, ed. 2002. *Voyages and Travels in the Near East During the Nineteenth Century*. Connecticut: Martino Publishing. Orig. pub. 1952.

Wheeler, Mortimer, ed. 1963. *Swans Hellenic Cruises: Handbook for 1963 Cruises*. London: Swan.

Whelpton, Barbara. 1954. *A Window on Greece*. London: Heinemann.

Whelpton, Eric, and Barbara Whelpton. 1961. *Greece and the Islands*. London: The Travel Book Club.

Wigram, W. A. 1947. *Hellenic Travel*. London: Faber.

Wills, David. 2005a. "British Accounts of Residency in Greece 1945-2004." *Journal of Modern Greek Studies* 23:177-97.

—. 2005b. "Contrasting Fortunes: The Reception of Athens and Sparta within Travel Writing of the Mid-Twentieth Century." *Studies in Travel Writing* 9:159-84.

—. 2006. "Ancient Sites, Modern Eyesores? The Transformation of the City of Athens in English-Language Accounts (1945-2005)." *Κάμπος: Cambridge Papers in Modern Greek* 14:103-27.

Winkler, Martin M. ed. 2001. *Classical Myth and Culture in the Cinema.* Oxford: Oxford University Press.

Woodhouse, C. M. 1976. *The Struggle for Greece, 1941-1949.* London: Granada.

Wordsworth, Christopher. 2004. *Athens and Attica: Journal of a Residence There.* Oxford: Archaeopress. Orig. pub. 1836.

Yalouri, Helen Anastasia [Eleana]. 1993. *Classical or Byzantine Heritage? Conflicting Pasts in Modern Greek Society.* M.Phil. diss., University of Cambridge.

Yalouri, Eleana. 2001. *The Acropolis: Global Fame, Local Claim.* Oxford: Berg.

Youngs, Tim. 1994. *Travellers in Africa: British Travelogues 1850-1900.* Manchester: Manchester University Press.

Youngs, Tim. 1997. "Foreword." *Studies in Travel Writing* 1:v-vi.

Zimmern, Alfred. 1911. *The Greek Commonwealth.* 5th ed. 1931. Reprint, Oxford: Oxford University Press, 1961.

Zinovieff, Sofka. 2004. *Eurydice Street: A Place in Athens.* London: Granta.

INDEX